Dance Halls and Last Calls

The History of Texas Country Music

T0159248

Geronimo Treviño III

REPUBLIC OF TEXAS PRESS

Lanham • Boulder • New York • Toronto • Oxford

Published by Republic of Texas Press
An imprint of The Rowman & Littlefield Publishing Group, Inc.
4501 Forbes Boulevard, Suite 200
Lanham, MD 20706

Distributed by NATIONAL BOOK NETWORK

Library of Congress Cataloging-in-Publication Data

Treviño, Geronimo.
    Dance halls and last calls : a history of Texas country music /
Geronmio Treviño III.
        p. cm
    "Sources":p.
    Includes index.
    ISBN 1-55622-927-5
    1. Country music—Texas—History and criticism. 2. Music halls—Texas.
I. Title.
ML3524.T72 2002
792.7'09764—dc21   2002000463

Manufactured in the United States of America.

Contents

Contents

Contents

Contents

Contents

Foreword

I grew up musically and socially in the dance halls and outdoor patio/pavilions of Texas. My first experience was a dance at the Farmer's Daughter in San Antonio in 1973. At the time we were living in California and had released our first album *Comin' Right At Ya*. After that weekend we fell in love with Texas and its dance halls and decided to move here and settle down. It was a love affair that started that night and continues today. From Gruene Hall and Schroeder Hall to the Reo Palm Isle to Caravan clubs to unnamed and forgotten dance halls all over the state, the traditions of dance and music are still carried on and are an important part of Texas's social and cultural life. Geronimo's accounts are a wonderful collection of a really important and cherished part of Texas musical and cultural history!

Ray Benson

Acknowledgments

Special thanks go out to the people who gave me photos to use from their private collections. The Austin County Historical Commission provided valuable information and photographs on dance halls in their part of southeast Texas. They represent more dance halls per capita than any place in the world.

Thanks to Adolph Hofner, Junior Mitchan, Dorothy Daffan Yannuzzi, Ray Szcepanik, Casey Monahan, Roy Lee Brown, Hank Harrison, Wiley Alexander, Deborah Damstrom, Sharon Hartsell, Ginnie Bivona, the Castroville Chamber of Commerce, Shelly Lee Alley Jr., George Chambers, and David Zettner. Thanks to David Garcia Jr. and Barry Snell for their legal assistance in making this book possible. Passionate thanks go out to all the legends that motivated me to put this project together. Without these heroes, country music would be quite different today.

Special thanks go to my band members: Jeff Simonson, Tom Strauch, Larry Goff, Henry Witek, Dick Walker, Leon Langley, and Byron Zipp for giving me the opportunity to perform in many of these dance halls. I must not forget all the individuals who have shared some fun moments in these halls with me, especially David "Chico" Reese, Karl Katzer, Dub Suttle, and all the friends, family, and fans that have encouraged me in writing this book.

Also, thanks to a couple of hall owners who have believed in me throughout the past eleven years: John Oaks and Steve Laughlin. Thanks to Frank Jennings for his expert direction and to Ray Benson, Jet Fellows, and Kevin Coffey for sharing their love of country music and the dance halls. Thanks to my daughters Laura and Katherine for their encouragement and help with ideas and typing and to my mother, Gloria Treviño, and my sister, Stella Lopez, for their never ending love and support and to my dad, Geronimo Treviño Jr., who was always there for me. And last but not least I

Acknowledgments

would like to thank my wife, Judy, for helping with most of the photography in the book and for her countless hours in helping me put all this together.

Introduction

They have always caught your attention as you traveled the roads of small rural Texas towns, whether on vacation or just out for a Sunday drive. They take on a different look when the Texas sun turns its light on them. There are fond memories of growing up visiting these "shrines" with family and recalling one's first dance steps. They are a big part of Texas culture and Texas history—they are the dance halls of the Lone Star State. In a modern world today that has videos, DVDs, cable television, and state-of-the-art indoor movie theaters to compete against the family values that these halls are known for, they have become threatened.

In order to place these halls in their proper perspective, one must begin with the music that people flocked to hear. Texans have always played an important role in the development of country music. The first cowboy singers, first country music star, first million dollar seller, first phonographic recordings, first instrument innovations, first pioneers in radio and television, and first to develop new music forms all had ties to Texas.

The German and Czech immigrants brought with them their Old World habits. The dance hall/community center became a focal meeting place for their favorite pastime of dancing and listening to singing groups. It provided the medicine they needed from the rigors of farm work.

Czech immigrants to Texas, especially those from the region of Bohemia, brought with them polka music, which eventually became a standard part of the repertoire for German, Slovenian, Polish, and Mexican musical groups throughout the state.

Brass and string bands became popular, and the music became characterized by nationalities from particular regions in the state. String bands were the roots of western swing. Eck Robertson and Bob Wills contributed their breakdown fiddle playing to help identify the early beginnings of this American music style. Robertson's old-time folk playing established Texas style fiddling. In 1922 he

Early German Brass Band from New Braunfels

Music in German settlements initially began with singing societies (sangervereine) and singing leagues (sangerbunde) entertaining large gatherings in their community centers. String and brass bands would later perform in these halls to another favorite pastime brought to America by their ancestors—dancing. *Photo courtesy of Harold Friesenhahn whose uncle was in the band.*

teamed with fellow fiddler and Civil War veteran Henry C. Gilliland to record for the Victor Talking Machine Company in New York. This became the first commercialized country music recording.

Country music's first million seller and first recording star was a man who took his stage name from two West Texas towns. Vernon Dalhart, born Marion Try Slaughter in Jefferson, Texas, on April 6, 1883, studied music at the Dallas Conservatory of Music and began his recording career on Columbia in 1916. He later became Thomas Edison's top recording artist with his 1924 recording of Henry Whitter's "The Wreck of the Old 97" and "The Prisoner's Song." These two songs featuring guitar, harmonica, and vocals became monster hits. With Dalhart's success the real cowboy singers emerged.

Carl T. Sprague is considered the original singing cowboy to be on record. Born on May 10, 1885, in Houston, he learned cowboy songs

Jules Verne Allen
The Singing Cowboy and his Cowhands, WOAI (1933)

Texas bronc buster and composer, Allen's Victor recordings of 1928 and 1929 included "Home on the Range," "Little Joe," and "The Wrangler." Left to right: Curly Williams, Jules Verne Allen, Mark Tankersley, Lonnie Williams, Ben McCay, and singer Marian. *Photo courtesy of Curly Williams.*

growing up while working on ranches and sitting around campfires. A graduate of Texas A&M, his 1925 recording "When the Work's All Done This Fall," described a return back home to see Mama after ranch work was completed. It became the first big cowboy song, selling approximately 900,000 copies and opened doors for other true singing cowboys and composers: Jules Verne Allen, Ken Maynard, Stuart Hamblen, Red River Dave McEnery, Tex Ritter, Bill Boyd, and everyone's favorite cowboy singer Gene Autry. Singing about round-ups, tumbleweeds, and ranch work, these western singers glorified their music on film. Ken Maynard was the first singing cowboy to appear in movies when he starred in *Song of the Saddle* in 1930. Later

Bob Wills and Ernest Tubb made their debuts on the silver screen, but it was Gene Autry who would be best remembered as the most popular cowboy in film and for his big recording hits. Born Orvon Eugene Autry in Tioga, Texas, on September 29, 1907, his big break came in 1934 when he sang in a Ken Maynard feature *Old Santa Fe*. Autry's pleasing vocals in this guest spot caught the attention of movie executives, and not long afterwards he became America's number one matinee idol, as fans of all ages would fill theater seats to see his films. Broadway humorist, writer, and actor Will Rogers gave Autry some encouragement when he encountered the young telegraph relief operator strumming his guitar between breaks, working the four-to-midnight shift at a telegraph office in Chelsea, Oklahoma. Autry went on to star on television and is the only artist to ever

Gene Autry
Photo from Geronimo Treviño collection

achieve five singles each selling five million copies. He reportedly sold more than 100 million records and was featured in ninety-three movies. He was inducted into the Country Music Hall of Fame in 1969.

Two brothers, Karl and Hugh Farr, settled prominently with America's quintessential western vocal group, the Sons of the Pioneers. They brought their jazz, western songs, guitar, and fiddle to add to the Pioneers' close harmonies. Hugh, born in Llano on December 6, 1902, first joined the group in 1933 and blended his jazz cowboy fiddle style. Karl was born in Rochele on April 25, 1909, and soon followed in his brother's footsteps to add his guitar to the Pioneers. Ex-members included Leonard Slye (later to change his name to Roy Rogers) and Ken Curtis who portrayed Festus on the long running television show *Gunsmoke*. The Farr Brothers were inducted into the Country Music Hall of Fame with the Sons of the Pioneers in 1980.

State Capitol, Austin, May 30, 1969

Seated: Bob Wills (far left), Tex Ritter (third from left), Calvin Robert Tubb (far right, representing his brother Ernest Tubb). Receiving proclamation honoring the three for their contributions to American music. *Photo courtesy of Junior Mitchan.*

Roy Rogers' career followed Autry's as one of the biggest western stars of all time. They died just three months apart in 1998. Rogers and his wife, Dale Evans, enjoyed an illustrious movie, television, and recording career together. Evans was born Frances Smith in Uvalde, Texas, on October 31, 1912. She co-wrote their theme song "Happy Trails." She died at the age of eighty-eight on February 8, 2001.

Another famous Texan to become a recording and film star was Tex Ritter. His real name was Woodward Maurice Ritter. Born January 12, 1907, in Murvaul in Panola County, he first became interested in acting before beginning his recording career. Influenced by author and scholar J. Frank Dobie while attending school at the University of Texas, he went on to become one of the best-loved cowboys in film and music. Ritter sang the theme song in the classic 1953 western *High Noon*, which won an Academy Award for best musical score. His youngest son is actor John Ritter. Tex joined the Country Music Hall of Fame in 1964.

Dave McEnery, born in San Antonio in 1914, received his nickname after singing "Red River Valley" many times. Best known for composing songs that dealt with the latest news topics of the day, he was also a pioneer in early television when he made the first broadcast at the 1939 New York World's Fair. The World's Fair offered a vision of the future in state-of-the-art technologies, and Red River Dave was there to sing the first country song on this new media at thirty frames per second. Red River Dave died on January 15, 2002.

The "Father of Country Music," its first big star, Jimmie Rodgers spent his last years living in Kerrville and San Antonio. Despite his deep southern upbringing, he became identified with Texas. His music influenced future stars Milton Brown, Ernest Tubb, Lefty Frizzell, Willie Nelson, Adolph Hofner, Gene Autry, Bob Wills, Hank Williams, Merle Haggard, and countless other artists who still perform his music today. The historic Bristol recording sessions set up by field engineer and talent scout Ralph Peer for the RCA Victor Company in Bristol, Tennessee, came to glorify what was to become country music. Peer, setting up his recording gear on the upper floors of a former furniture store after newspaper advertisements lured the singers to him, had little idea what would come out of these sessions. Before the historical recordings, country music was termed hillbilly—string music. Jimmie Rodgers fused jazz and blues with folk to help define country music. Accompanying himself on guitar after a

Red River Dave McEnery
Photo courtesy of Hank Harrison

dispute with band members, his sessions were to soon capture the attention of a Depression era America. Singing railroad laborers became his first musical mentors. Their chants and ballads were later reflected in his songs. He related to the people across the nation with his self-penned songs that told of places and of people he loved to visit. "The Singing Brakeman" and "America's Blue Yodeler" became the singing sensation of the country; his music was the first to reach mass America. He died on May 26, 1933, after a long battle with tuberculosis and thirty-six hours after completing his final RCA recording in New York City. Rodgers was the first person to be inducted into the Country Music Hall of Fame in 1961.

Country music was revolutionized again when the Carter Family made their entrance to the temporary recording studios in Bristol just days apart from Rodgers'. Their close harmonies and songs about a rural America left a great musical impact on the nation as well. Their Texas connection was due to a 100,000-watt Mexican radio station

Jimmie Rodgers "The Father of Country Music"
Photo courtesy of Jimmie Dale Court

transmitting across the border in a studio in Del Rio, Texas. Station XERA was owned by Dr. John R. Brinkley, who once had a quack medical clinic in Kansas that offered goat gland transplants, which he claimed would aid the sexual energies of older men. Called a border blast station due to having up to ten times the transmission power of the largest clear channel in America, it enabled the Carter Family's music to quickly spread throughout the nation. From 1938-1941 Alvin Pleasant Carter with his wife, Sara, and their daughter Janette along with Mother Maybelle Carter (cousin to Sara who also married A.P.'s brother Ezra) with their daughters Helen, June, and Anita became a nationally popular act on this border station format. Sara sang lead while playing guitar or autoharp, and Maybelle played lead guitar. Their close harmonies on ballads, blues, and gospel songs represented rural America well. The first family of country music chose to live in San Antonio rather than Del Rio, and they would spend the winters in Texas avoiding the harsh climate in their home state of Virginia. Electronic transcriptions were made in a garage and then sent to the border station in Del Rio for broadcasting at a later date. These types of recordings were made popular by advertisers when distributing the various products they were promoting. Credit the Carter Family for bringing us such country standards as "Can the Circle be Unbroken" and "Wildwood Flower."

Prince Albert Hunt, from Terrell, Texas, is a forgotten pioneer who bridged the gap between breakdown fiddle and the beginnings of western swing. Hunt led one of the first string bands to include a vocalist. He was killed by his girlfriend's husband after leaving a Dallas dance hall in 1931.

Bandleader, fiddler, and songwriter Shelly Lee Alley, born July 6, 1894, in Colorado County, was one of the first bandleaders to broadcast on early radio (WFAA) in Dallas. He recorded a self-penned song "Travelin' Blues" in San Antonio with Jimmie Rodgers in 1931. The twin fiddles of Alley and his brother Alvin on the recording later opened up the eyes and ears of Bob Wills. A year later Rogers would record another Alley composition titled "Gambling Barroom Blues." The following is an article that appeared in the November 1994 issue of *The Journal of Country Music* by country music writer Kevin Coffey.

Shelly Lee Alley is a puzzle of contradictions and half-ful-filled promise. As the writer of Jimmie Rodgers' classic "Travelin' Blues," as an early exponent of western swing, and as a star of early Texas radio, he looms as something more than a footnote in country music history. But how much more? That question goes to the heart of his frus-trating career.

A pop musician, songwriter, and bandleader who veered toward hillbilly music at mid-career, but who seems not entirely to have come to terms with the implications of that move, Alley elicits both veneration and disappoint-ment from those familiar with his music. His recorded blues and hokum hold up well today, fine examples of free-wheeling, good time dance music of the Depression years, while his ballads on record, at least, fare far less well. Alley himself retained little affection for the risqué blues and stomps, dying frustrated that what he felt were his best songs were left either unrecorded or unreleased.

What was recorded and released is a bizarre mix, its wide divergences captured pointedly in the lyrics—from one of his strongest ballads and one of his most typical off-color blues. Commercial and artistic considerations often clashed; his songwriting was characterized on one hand by a cloying sentimentality fostered in the more inno-cent times before the First World War and on the other by a cynical, Jazz Age hedonism unrelenting preoccupied with sex and beer joint carousing.

Clyde Brewer, a music legend himself and step-son of Alley, recalls stories told by his Uncle Alvin of the time Jimmie Rodgers stopped by to pick up the two brothers on their journey to record in San Antonio. The ride from Ramsey, Texas, in Colorado County must have been quite an adventure, as Rodgers sped through narrow coun-try roads in his custom-built Cadillac with the Alley brothers in tow. Little did they know that the real adventure awaited them in a make-shift recording studio at the Texas Hotel in San Antonio. On January 31, 1931, "Travelin' Blues" was recorded and soon became a consid-erable hit and was instrumental in aiding the careers of Shelly and Alvin.

Shelly Lee Alley and His Alley Cats

Shelly Lee Alley pictured far right and a very young Floyd Tillman on far left with their Texas Centennial hats. *Photo courtesy of Shelly Lee Alley Jr.*

In Jimmie Rodgers' biography by Nolan Porterfield titled *Jimmie Rodgers: The Life and Times of America's Blue Yodler,* he gives his view on the famous recording session: "'Travelin' Blues' brought together, in however a rudimentary a fashion, the strains of several musical traditions, notably jazz-blues and those elements of popular music most directly derived from older, folk roots."

The Texas music of western swing was about to explode in the Southwest. The combination of jazz, fiddle breakdowns, pop, blues, Dixieland, and the big band sound were soon to be heard in dance halls and on commercial radio. Record companies felt that radio would hinder the marketing of their products if heard on the airwaves so bands performed "live" during this golden era of radio. This allowed bands the opportunity to plug the shows they were to play in the immediate area.

Bob Wills and Milton Brown became the driving force behind the development of western swing, and the music form took on a more defined category.

James Robert Wills, born in Limestone County on March 6, 1905, first met Brown at a house dance, and they started performing together in medicine shows. This led to the formation of the Aladdin Laddies, where in addition to playing dances, they would promote Aladdin Kerosene Lamps on radio. Shortly afterwards in 1930, they became known as the Light Crust Doughboys after securing a sponsorship with Light Crust Flour (an important staple in a Depression era America). The Burrus Mill and Elevator Company, makers of Light Crust Flour, was managed by the ambitious Wilbert "Pappy" Lee O'Daniel who became governor of Texas in 1938 and also served a stint in the United States Senate. The Doughboys first performed on radio station KFJZ out of Fort Worth around January of 1931 and became an instant success. This allowed Brown the opportunity to promote his dances on the airwaves, the first to take advantage of this. They soon moved to a more powerful 50,000-watt station, WBAP, and could now be heard throughout the Southwest. After the band recorded for Victor Records in February of 1932, they became known as the Fort Worth Doughboys. In 1932 Brown resigned from the Doughboys after O'Daniel forced the band to quit playing dances

Original Light Crust Doughboys KFJZ Radio, Fort Worth, January 1931

Sponsored by Light Crust Flour From left: Bob Wills (fiddle), Truett Kimzey (announcer), Milton Brown (vocals) and Herman Arnspiger (guitar). *Photo courtesy of Smokey Montgomery and Roy Lee Brown.*

and refused to put Brown's brother Derwood on salary. Brown was replaced by vocalist Tommy Duncan, and Wills remained with the Doughboys for another year.

Brown immediately formed his own group, the Musical Brownies. Brown's star status was huge, and his importance to western swing cannot be overlooked. His innovations are immeasurable. He organized the first western swing band and was the first to add twin fiddles and a jazz pianist (Fred "Papa" Calhoun). The sweet pop-oriented vocals of Brown characterized the band. Brown had been singing jazz and pop tunes at regular dances at Crystal Springs Dance Pavilion since 1930. One can pinpoint the beginning of western swing at Crystal Springs, which was located four miles northwest of

Milton Brown "The Father of Western Swing"
Photo courtesy of Roy Lee Brown

Light Crust Doughboys, October 5, 1933

Standing: W. Lee "Pappy" O'Daniel Inside car left to right: Henry Stein Barre (driver), Sleepy Johnson (piano/guitar), Ramon D'Armon (bass/vocals), Leon McCauliffe (steel guitar), Leon Hoff (vocals/guitar), Cliff Gross (fiddle), and Herman Arnspiger (guitar). *Photo courtesy of Smokey Montgomery.*

downtown Fort Worth on White Settlement Road. It also served as great training ground for Brown's unique music innovations. Willie Milton Brown, born in Stephenville on September 8, 1903, became a link between the rural and urban audiences by introducing vocals to string bands. First using megaphones to project his lyrics, around 1930 he experimented in using a public address system. Generators were used to amplify band instruments before electricity provided by the Rural Electric Association made it economical and possible to project above crowd noise. Brown would introduce his western swing, which was labeled "hillbilly string music." It took the name western swing several years later. He added a steel guitar in his band when he hired Bob Dunn, who became the first country music artist to play an electrically amplified instrument when he recorded with Brown in 1935. Brown also brought to country music one of the first band buses to travel marketing their band's name. Brown died in 1936 from complications due to pneumonia brought on by an automobile accident on the Jacksboro Highway five days earlier. "The Founder of

Milton Brown and his Musical Brownies (WBAP, Fort Worth)
Photo probably taken in early 1936

From left: Wanna Coffman (bass), Cecil Brower (fiddle), Bob Dunn (steel guitar), Cliff Bruner (fiddle), Fred Calhoun (piano), Milton Brown (vocals), Ocie Stockard (banjo), and Derwood Brown (guitar). *Photo courtesy of Roy Lee Brown.*

Western Swing" continues to influence generations of musicians long after his death.

The following is a paragraph from the well written and researched book *Milton Brown and the Founding of Western Swing*, by Cary Ginell with assistance from Brown's youngest brother, Roy Lee Brown.

> Crystal Springs may have helped make Milton Brown the King of Fort Worth, but it was the touring, the nightly trek to the small hamlets, sleepy towns and occasional big cities that secured the Musical Brownies' place in Texas's musical history. An additional by-product of the Brownies' success with the public was their influence on countless other organizations bent on duplicating their fame. Although none approached the Brownies' overall popularity during Milton's lifetime, many groups used the Musical Brownies as a model, copying their style, repertoire, wardrobe and instrumentation.

Brown and Wills fused the big band sound with jazz, blues, folk, Dixieland, mariachi, and pop to create a sound that was limited to the Southwest in the beginning. Difficulty in air and car travel during the Depression made way for this region of America to learn of this music form on radio and nearby dance halls. Wills continued to popularize this music form in dance halls and on radio to become the "King of Western Swing." Gangsters Bonnie Parker, Clyde Barrow, and Pretty Boy Floyd were patrons who often attended Doughboy dances in Fort Worth at Crystal Springs Dance Hall. Controversial Spade Cooley would make his mark in California, but it was Wills' longevity and popularity that labeled him the "King of Western Swing."

Shortly after the Light Crust Doughboys began broadcasting on radio in 1931, O'Daniel fired the band because he did not like "hillbilly music." The popularity of the group was becoming established as cards and letters poured in from listeners and demanded their return. They were quickly hired back. O'Daniel soon saw an increased sales in Burrus Flour and became the announcer for the show as well as the band's manager. The show was syndicated on radio stations in San Antonio, Houston, and Oklahoma. Wills left the Doughboys in 1934 after a dispute with O'Daniel, but not without controversy from the future governor of Texas. The Playboys were actually first established in Waco after Wills took vocalist Tommy Duncan, banjo playing younger brother Johnnie Lee Wills, and the Whalin brothers, June and Kermit, to broadcast shows on radio station WACO and play in dance halls around Central Texas.

Wills moved to Oklahoma City to begin broadcasting on WKY. The band was now billed as Bob Wills and his Texas Playboys for the first time. Along this journey, before settling down in Oklahoma, there was always the nemesis of O'Daniel to stir things up for Wills. While Wills was in Waco, O'Daniel sued Wills (he lost) for marketing the phrase "former Light Crust Doughboys" on posters that advertised their dance hall dates, and he made it difficult for Wills to secure his initial radio show in Oklahoma City, later finding a home on radio station KVOO in Tulsa. The nine years the Texas Playboys spent at KVOO were their most successful.

When Bob Wills took his Texas Playboys to perform on the Grand Ole Opry in Nashville, he insisted on using drums, despite negative concerns from Opry officials (tenor banjos were first used as rhythm instruments). Before long, drummers were allowed on the Grand Ole

Opry. Wills helped introduce not only drums to country music but popularized electric instruments as well. The western outfits and use of a tour bus by the Playboys changed the way Nashville would view country performers. Bob Wills was inducted into the Country Music Hall of Fame in 1968. He was also inducted into the Rock and Roll Hall of Fame in 1999 in the "early influence" category that includes artists whose music predates rock and roll, but who inspired and had a profound effect on rock and roll music.

L to R: Wills, Governor Preston Smith, Harvey Frazier, and Junior Mitchan. This is Bob Wills' last public appearance before his stroke. He had received a proclamation honoring him for his accomplishments in country music. This photo was taken at the state capitol in Austin on May 30, 1969, at 3:30 p.m. Wills had a stroke that night in Fort Worth. *Photo courtesy of Junior Mitchan.*

During the 1920s and 1930s the Riverside Dance Hall, located just outside of Leakey, Texas, featured the big band sound of the Black Diamonds, an all-black band from San Antonio. The hall immediately closed after a man and his three sons wrestled a handgun away from a Texas Ranger and shot him in the back. Courts could never prove which man actually pulled the trigger. At another location a few miles south of Riverside Hall where dances were held at the Rio Frio schoolhouse, a Mexican man watched the activity from outside through windows of the schoolhouse. Although not allowed inside to experience the fun, he was just as entertained by the fun that went on with certain couples spending precious moments together in their automobiles.

The development of conjunto music was another music form that came out of Texas. Conjunto music originated in the late 1800s after inexpensive duty-free German- and Italian-made one-row button accordions became available in the border regions along the Rio Grande River. German and Czech immigrants entering the Gulf Coast area of Texas introduced their musical styles, and their music quickly spread and found its way into rural communities. The addition of the bajo sexto (twelve-string guitar) was the final ingredient that established the conjunto sound and allowed the accordion to become the lead instrument. The rancheras and corridos (ballads) spoke of the common folk, and the accordion became the instrument of the people. Ranch hands and field workers embraced this art form because it sent a message about the hardships they endured, and racial conflict to Anglo domination became a major theme. The folk roots of conjunto are equivalent to the hillbilly roots that formed country music. Santiago Jimenez Sr., credited as the "Father" of modern conjunto music, was a pioneer accordionist and songwriter who took German and Czech influenced accordion and created his own Mexican-American sound that his sons Leonardo "Flaco" and Santiago Jimenez Jr. have carried on. Santiago Sr. attended dances with his father, Patricio, a seven-foot accordion player from Eagle Pass, and learned traditional European dance songs.

One of the most important blues musicians of all time took a detour to Texas in 1936. Robert Johnson, born in 1911 near Hazelhurst, Mississippi, recorded three different sessions at the Gunter Hotel in San Antonio. The sixteen songs he laid down represent some of the most influential songs in the history of popular music. Johnson had caught the attention of Ernie Oertle, a representative for the American Record Company, who had heard of his legendary skills and recruited him for the sessions. This Delta Blues pioneer was to later have an enormous impact on artists such as Bob Dylan and Eric Clapton. Clapton made Johnson known to millions of new fans when he recorded "Cross Road Blues" in 1968. It became a worldwide hit and stirred up new interest in Johnson.

Santiago Jimenez Sr. and Sus Valedores
Photo courtesy of Santiago Jimenez Jr.

Johnson mysteriously died in 1938 at the young age of twenty-seven after drinking whiskey from a bottle that contained poison. As legend goes, he had befriended a woman at a roadhouse outside Greenwood, Mississippi, whose husband was the proprietor of the establishment. Jealousy would end his life. The United States Postal Service issued a stamp commemorating Johnson. He continues to be one of America's best-known blues icons.

Texas was the home to four blues pioneers who created some of the finest music about rural and urban America. Blind Lemon Jefferson, born blind in Coutchman in July 1897 (estimated date), recorded close to one hundred songs between 1926 and 1929. He was a major influence on Robert Johnson, Lightnin' Hopkins, and Louis Armstrong. He was one of Black America's most popular blues artists of the day.

Delta Blues Pioneer Robert Johnson

His blues recordings at the Gunter Hotel in San Antonio, Texas, became some of the most influential songs in the history of popular music. *Original art by Geronimo Treviño.*

Huddie "Leadbelly" Ledbetter moved to Texas with his family at the age of five, growing up in the Caddo Lake region of East Texas. He learned his music through cotton field workers and spirituals. He traveled with Blind Lemon Jefferson playing music together after meeting one another in the Deep Ellum district of Dallas. "Goodnight Irene" and "The Midnight Special" (written while in prison in Sugar Land for murder) are two standards that Leadbelly left us.

Mance Lipscomb, born April 9, 1895, in Navasota, began his recording career at the age of sixty-five. Muddy Waters and Bob Dylan were a few of his many fans.

The folk-blues revival of the early 1960s gained new fans for Sam "Lightnin" Hopkins when he was rediscovered by record producer Sam Charters. Born in Centerville, Texas, on March 15, 1912, he was a musical hero to Texas songwriter Townes Van Zandt.

Adolph Hofner, whose career spanned over sixty years, always made customers feel welcome whenever they came out to his dances. He would remember a name or maybe a couple's favorite song. Some of the music he played came from his German and Czech ancestry and was influenced by the Bohemian dance bands he grew up listening to. He sang songs in Czech and blended polkas, waltzes, schottisches, western swing, and country. Known as the "Bing Crosby of country music," he credits Milton Brown for the inspiration to keep singing. Born on June 8, 1916, in Moulton, he teamed with his brother Emil "Bash" Hofner and first performed in San Antonio in the 1930s.

In 1936 they both joined the Jimmie Revard band and then did a stint with Tom Dickie and the Showboys before forming Adolph and the Boys in 1938. Two recordings helped propel Adolph's career. He scored a regional hit with "Maria Elena" under the moniker Adolph and the San Antonians, and his recording of "Cotton-Eyed Joe," the first on record, became a national hit in 1941. With the sponsorship of the Pearl Beer Company in the 1950s, Adolph changed the name of his band for the last time. Adolph Hofner and the Pearl Wranglers continued to perform until the 1990s. He led one of the longest running bands in country music. He died on June 2, 2000. They played Fischer Hall, Cherry Springs Hall, Pat's Hall, and London Hall on a regular touring schedule. Adolph stated that Fischer Hall was where he actually took off professionally. Later in his long career he performed at The Farmer's Daughter every Wednesday for twenty-five

Jimmie Revard and his Oklahoma Playboys, KTSA Radio, 1937

Left to right: George Timberlake, Jimmie Revard, Curly Williams, Bob Bellmard, Adolph Hofner, Chet Carnes, Emil "Bash" Hofner, Cal Callison, and unknown announcer. *Photo courtesy of Hank Harrison.*

Tom Dickey and The Showboys (1940) WOAI Radio

Left to right: Bill Dickey, Walter Kleypas, Tom Dickey, Curly Williams, and Joe Grant. *Photo courtesy of Curly Williams.*

Adolph Hofner and the Pearl Wranglers

Battle of Flowers Parade, San Antonio, Texas, early 1950s. *Photo courtesy of Hank Harrison.*

years. Resentment of his name during World War II forced him to go by "Dolf." Only three letters separated his name from Adolph Hitler.

Rain and rutted roads made travel more difficult, but whenever he saw the dancers come out on the floor it made him feel good. Cover charge was thirty-five cents for men when he first started performing, and ladies were admitted free of charge. Many of his dances went from sundown to sunup. In 1932 or 1933, while playing in a club in San Antonio at the corner of Broadway and Alamo Street (down the street working for tips at The Big Nickel was Ernest Tubb), a young singer/songwriter/guitarist approached Adolph and asked if he could perform between band breaks. "We couldn't believe what we were hearing; his music and guitar work left us speechless," remembered Adolph, in his Czech accent. The young man's name was Floyd Tillman, and he would soon become one of the originators of the honky-tonk sound.

Born on December 8, 1914, and raised in Post, Texas, Tillman was one of the first songwriters to write about the subject of infidelity. Considered one of the first country artists to record with an electric guitar (with the Blue Ridge Playboys in 1936), his half-spoken vocal style sliding and looping into notes was unique. He wrote "It Makes No Difference Now" and had offered it to Adolph for the sum of ten dollars, but at that time he showed no interest in it. Singer/songwriter and future Louisiana governor Jimmie Davis purchased it for three hundred dollars (later Tillman re-acquired the rights) and it became a huge hit for Cliff Bruner, Gene Autry, and Bing Crosby.

After a short stint with Hofner, Tillman moved to Houston in 1934. His experience playing the mandolin with his musical brothers led to his "take off guitar style." He scored his first hit song "They Took the Stars Out of Heaven" after being signed to the Decca label in 1942. A second hit followed two years later when he recorded "Each Night at Nine." He soon scored hit songs with a Jerry Irby tune titled "Nails in My Coffin," and later "I Love You So Much it Hurts" and "Slippin' Around" were two of his songs that he became identified with.

Kevin Coffey's liner notes in *The Daffan Records Story* gives the following description of Floyd: "Tillman is a true product of his state's rich musical heritage, having absorbed jazz, blues, country and various ethnic influences and molded them into a highly individual style." At Tillman's eighty-fifth birthday celebration at the Lan-Tex Theater in Llano, Texas, Willie Nelson proclaimed Floyd Tillman the greatest country songwriter alive today. Tillman was inducted into the Country Music Hall of Fame in 1984.

Some of the most important and influential pioneers in country music came from the Houston area. Leon "Pappy" Selph, born April 7, 1914, in Houston, was a fiddler, bandleader, and another pioneer of western swing and Texas country music. He formed the Blue Ridge Playboys (named after oil-rich Blue Ridge, Texas) in 1934 and had the distinction of having band members that became the nucleus for developing the honky-tonk sound. Together Floyd Tillman with Moon Mullican and Ted Daffan mixed western swing and honky-tonk that Al Dexter and Ernest Tubb later contributed to.

Floyd Tillman (1948)
Photo courtesy of Mrs. J. R. Chatwell

Ted Daffan's career spanned over forty years, but he continued to write and publish songs until his death in 1996. As a bandleader, he was innovative in using lead guitar as the foremost instrument along with his accomplished steel guitar work. This was a big departure from the fiddle-dominated sound of most country bands. His most prominent recordings were with his band Ted Daffan and His Texans, and he is known today as a leading songwriter with such standards as "Born to Lose" (written after an all-night poker game), "No Letter Today," "Worried Mind," and "I'm a Fool to Care."

Daffan wrote the first song to honor the truck driver with "Truck Driver Blues" recorded by Cliff Bruner. The record appealed to listeners of the then-new jukebox, which was placed in truck stops and taverns around the country. A look into Daffan's set list gives an excellent indication as to what songs were being played in dance halls in the late 1940s and early 1950s. Besides his own compositions he

Ted Daffan and His Texans (January 1940)

First Recording Band. Left to right: Buddy Buller (electric guitar), Ralph C. "Smitty" Smith (piano), Ted Daffan (lap steel guitar), Chuck Keeshan (rhythm guitar), Harry Sorenson (accordion), and Elmer B. Christian (bass). *Photo courtesy of Ted's daughter Dorothy Daffan Yannuzzi.*

Ted Daffan
Photo courtesy of Dorothy Daffan Yannuzzi

selected material written by Jimmie Rodgers, Moon Mullican, Ernest Tubb, A.P. Carter, Lefty Frizzell, Floyd Tillman (they were best friends), Bob Wills, Cindy Walker, and Leon Payne. Daffan died on October 6, 1996.

Country music has been blessed with many extraordinary songwriters. It would be difficult to make a decision as to who is the top songwriter of all time, but if one were pressured to do so, the name Cindy Walker would come to mind. Born in Mart, Texas, on July 20, 1918, Walker's first big break resulted when she managed to demo her song "Lone Star Trail" to Bing Crosby. He recorded it in 1941. Gene Autry, Al Dexter, Ernest Tubb, Eddy Arnold, Jim Reeves, Roy Orbison, and Bob Wills all recorded her tunes. Her biggest songs included "Cherokee Maiden," "You Don't Know Me," "I Don't Care," "In the Misty Moonlight," "Take Me in Your Arms and Hold Me," and "Distant Drums." Walker was inducted into the Country Music Hall of Fame in 1997.

Leon Payne, known as "The Blind Balladeer," was born in Alba on June 15, 1917. He wrote the country standards "I Love You Because" and "You've Still Got a Place in My Heart" and Hank Williams' hits "They'll Never Take Her Love From Me" and "Lost Highway." Payne and Williams remained the closest of friends. He recorded for Bluebird, Bullet, Decca, and Capitol record labels and also played in Bob Wills' band in 1938. Payne passed away in 1969.

Clifton Lafayette Bruner, born in Texas City on April 25, 1915, was the last living member of Milton Brown's Musical Brownies. He was yet another main contributor to western swing and honky-tonk. Bruner played on close to three hundred recordings and had scheduled a session just before his death on August 25, 2000. He has been a major influence to most of the fiddle players in Texas. Jazz fiddler and former Texas Playboy Johnny Gimble claims Bruner as one of his idols. Bruner recalled that when he first started playing professionally at the age of fourteen or fifteen, you could rent a room for fifteen to twenty cents, and a good lunch would cost you fifteen cents. Mexican food was a nickel cheaper. "When I joined Milton Brown at the age of twenty, he took me from hamburgers to steaks," remembered Bruner. Bruner and His Texas Wanderers band were the first to record "It Makes No Difference Now" featuring vocalist Dickie McBride for Decca Records, and presses ran nonstop for two weeks to keep up with record sales. It sold millions of copies and was recorded in eight

Leon Payne
Photo courtesy of Mrs. Murtie Payne

different languages.

Cliff Bruner and the Texas Wanderers were extremely popular in Houston and eventually moved to Beaumont where they performed on radio shows three times daily. The Wanderers consisted of Bob Dunn on steel guitar, singer and guitarist Dickie McBride, pioneer mandolin player Leo Raley (the first to electrify a mandolin), piano player and singer Moon Mullican, and bass player Hezzy Bryant. Bruner's freewheeling jazz playing had no boundaries, and his improvisations became his style.

Cliff Bruner and the Texas Wanderers 1938, Beaumont

Left to right, standing: Rip Ramsey (bass), Morris Gleason (banjo), Cliff Bruner (fiddle), Elmer Goodman (bus driver), J.R. Chatwell (fiddle), and Morris Deason (guitar) Seated: Alton Durden (steel guitar) and Max Bennett (piano). *Photo courtesy of Mrs. J.R. Chatwell.*

A businessman by the name of Matt Honk who sold pianos to saloons in the old west is credited with the term honky-tonk. It was first used by players of ragtime as an allusion to his name. The 1941 movie *Honky-Tonk* starring Clark Gable also helped popularize the name.

Al Dexter (Clarence Albert Poindexter), born in Jacksonville in

1902, was the first person to use the term in song in 1935 when he recorded "Honky-Tonk Blues." Dexter's songs about honky-tonk life came from true experiences he learned from playing in roadhouses and from engagements at his own honky-tonk called the Roundup Club in Turnertown. A gun-toting woman chasing her husband's girl-friend (who happened to be a waitress at the Roundup) was the inspiration for his song "Pistol Packing Mama" that was later covered by Bing Crosby. The song went to number one on both the pop and country charts. Decca Records was one of the first companies to market country songs on both formats.

Moon Mullican (Aubrey Mullican), born in Corrigan on March 29, 1909, was a master of western swing music and was a major influence to rhythm and blues artists with his jump beat piano playing. Known as the "King of the Hillbilly Piano," he left Pappy Selph to join Cliff Bruner's Texas Wanderers and record for Decca.

Fiddle virtuoso Caesare Masse gave some insight as to what it

Another band that called themselves the Texas Playboys
is shown in the late 1930s (photo taken in Pearland, Texas,
at the Wander Tavern named after Cliff Bruner's band)

Left to right: Herman Stanley (guitar), Caesare Masse (fiddle), Leo Herbert (mandolin), Tiny Moore (bass), Don Tyler (guitar), and Jack Achtley (piano). *Photo courtesy of Junior Mitchan.*

was like traveling from town to town playing dance halls. Born in a gypsy camp close to Tyler on March 29, 1909, Caesare worked with Adolph Hofner, Cliff Bruner, Hoyle Nix, and Arkey Blue. His haunting jazz fiddle was heard in dance halls for eight decades. On a trip with Moon Mullican and the Delmore Brothers during a Texas tour in the 1940s Caesare recalled what life could be like on the road.

Brothers Alton and Rabon, a popular duet act from Alabama (inducted into the Hall of Fame in 2001), were known for their complex harmonies in country music. Caesare recalled that the brothers would sometimes find religion during a drinking spree. Each had their own bottle of whiskey and they would take turns toasting to the Lord. Alton would ask, "Brother Rabon, do you suppose that God would mind if I drank the rest of this whiskey?" Rabon responded, "Let's give our hearts to God and drink to him." Moon and Caesare were trying their best to not laugh at the brothers as they continued to raise their whiskey bottles toward the sky. Suddenly Rabon started to feel sick from all of the whiskey he had consumed and pleaded to stop the truck they were riding in. Alton grabbed Rabon's head and held it out the door as he began to throw up. In a puny voice he begged his brother to pray for him because he felt as if he was "gonna die." Alton, speaking in a thick Alabama drawl, asked God to please help his brother because he was so drunk. Rabon turned to Alton and said, "Don't tell him I'm drunk, tell him I'm just sick."

Another western swing pioneer whose name may not be as recognizable as others but is still talked about in music circles in Texas is J.R. "Chat the Cat" Chatwell. Born in Stamford, Texas, on May 27, 1915, J.R. (initials being his real name) may not have attained worldly recognition, but his fiddle style is greatly respected in Texas. Combining breakdowns, blues, and hot jazzy licks, he was an explosive and exciting fiddle player. Over the years he played with Adolph Hofner's various bands, The Hi-Flyers, Cliff Bruner (who hired J.R. for his first professional job), The Modern Mountaineers, The Light Crust Doughboys, Uncle John Wills' Band, Dickie McBride and the Village Boys, Smiley Whitley's Texans, and Walter Kleypas' Lone Star Band. He and Bruner were major contributors to western swing. J.R. Chatwell died in 1983.

Here is a look into one of his nights out on the road. After traveling from an engagement late one morning, he decided to pull off the road and get a little rest. In doing so he parked his car on an incline by

Adolph Hofner and J.R. Chatwell

Left to right: J.R. Chatwell (fiddle), Adolph Hofner (guitar), Fritz (drums), and Emil "Bash" Hofner (steel guitar) performing in 1951 at Mansfield Park in Bandera. *Photo courtesy of Mrs. J.R. Chatwell.*

the shoulder of the road and propped up against the back door of his vehicle and did not awaken until a highway patrolman inspecting the vehicle opened the door and J.R. came crashing out. Suffering from a bit of a hangover, he immediately started cussing and raising hell until he focused on the patrolman. "Hi, my name is J.R. Chatwell," he enthusiastically responded to the officer.

In Frankie McWhorter's *Cowboy Fiddler*, he recalls his time on the road playing fiddle for Bob Wills. The Texas Playboys had been playing some clubs in California when their bus broke down and instruments had to be transported in a rented covered trailer. A particular band member whose duty was to watch over Wills was invited to go on a fishing trip on their day off. Wills had been on a drinking binge, and not wanting to cancel the fishing trip, the "baby-sitter" loaded a passed-out Bob Wills into the trailer and locked the door. Wills awoke when the car stopped for refueling, and he immediately started to bang on the trailer. The filling station attendant noted that someone was in the trailer, and one of the band members explained that they were working for the California Insane Asylum and were transporting a patient who thinks he's Bob Wills. The attendant ignored Wills pleas for help and told one of the band members "You know, that son of a gun is crazy. He does think he's Bob Wills."

Texas Troubadour Ernest Tubb took the honky-tonk sound to another level when he first performed on the Grand Ole Opry stage in

Ernest Tubb, The Texas Troubadour
Photo courtesy of Hank Harrison

1943. Born February 9, 1914, in Crisp, Texas, he started his music career working for KONO Radio in San Antonio beginning in 1934. It is hard to picture the lanky Ernest Tubb riding his bicycle to the radio station each morning with his guitar strapped on his back, but this is what he had to do. Tubb's idol was Jimmie Rodgers, and Carrie Rodgers (Jimmie's widow) was instrumental in helping launch his career. She helped him secure a recording contract with Bluebird Records (a subsidiary of Decca), recording in 1936 at the Texas Hotel in San Antonio. In these makeshift recording studios, beds and mattresses from the hotel were usually placed against the windows to better the sound on the recordings. His first big hit was on Decca when he recorded the classic "Walking the Floor Over You." This was the song that propelled him to the Opry. The danceable music of honky-tonk mixed with a driving electric and steel guitar took America by storm. Tubb's career lasted a half-century, and he was the first honky-tonk singer to achieve national recognition. He first experimented with the lead guitar; it became the key instrument in his band at the E & E Tavern, a club he owned in San Angelo, Texas. With jukeboxes being played in beer joints and roadhouses all over the Southwest, the electric guitar was needed to overpower other instruments while records spinned and cut through patron's voices. Tubb also pioneered the first record shop after fans complained they had difficulty obtaining his recordings. The Ernest Tubb Record Shop was established in Nashville, and for the first time country music records were made available to the public through mail order; the record shop continues to meet the public's demands today. Tubb was made a member of the Country Music Hall of Fame in 1965. He died in 1984.

The postwar period gave way to more of the honky-tonk sound as it was being played in dance halls, roadhouses, and beer joints all over the state.

Lefty Frizzell, born William Orville Frizzell on March 3, 1928, in Corsicana, Texas, is perhaps the most influential country singer and songwriter of all time. His vocal style of holding on to syllables and his unique phrasing has been imitated by many country vocalists and continues to influence country singers today. He is the only artist to have had four country songs in the top ten at one time (1951). His song "That's the Way Love Goes," co-written with Sanger "Whitey" Shafer, charted number one twice with Johnny Rodriguez in 1973 and ten years later with Merle Haggard. Shafer, born in Whitney, Texas, also co-wrote "I Never Go Around Mirrors" with Frizzell, one of the most heart wrenching country songs ever written. Frizzell was the first country singer to wear rhinestones onstage. He lived the songs he recorded. He entered the Country Music Hall of Fame in 1972.

Kevin Coffey gives his observation on developments on the music scene after the 1940s.

> The 1950s are generally seen as declining years for Western Swing and this was certainly true for the music's most famous exponents Bob Wills and his Texas Playboys. It was especially true in the latter half of the decade, when rock and roll burst onto the scene and altered America's musical landscape. But even earlier in the decade, television, changing tastes and a changing economy had toppled the music from its mid-to-late forties peak of popularity. Still, the music flourished in pockets and its influence was readily apparent not only in honky-tonk and mainstream country, but also in rockabilly and rock and roll.

The twangy, rock influenced honky-tonk style known as the Bakersfield sound is traced to Buck Owens and Merle Haggard. Owens, born Alvis Edgar Owens, in Sherman, Texas, on August 12, 1929, had fifteen number one hits in the mid-1960s and became a popular figure on the country comedy show *Hee Haw*. Owens was inducted into the Country Music Hall of Fame in 1996 along with Ray Price.

In the words of Kris Kristofferson, when presenting the Country Music Hall of Fame award to Ray Noble Price, "Ray Price is the living link between Hank Williams and the country music of today." Kristofferson, Willie Nelson, Roger Miller, Hank Cochran, Harlon Howard, and Bill Anderson owe the start of their own songwriting careers to Price for recording many of their classic songs. Born in Perryville, Cherokee County, Texas, on January 12, 1926, Price's 4/4 shuffles defined country music, and his crooning smooth vocals have made him one of country music's best voices of all time. Price was a one-time roommate of Hank Williams. Band members in his Cherokee Cowboy Band built new careers like actors from popular television sitcoms. Roger Miller, Willie Nelson, Johnny Bush, and Darrell McCall were all in Price's band at one time. His 1956 recording of "Crazy Arms," which was on the charts for forty-five weeks, helped establish him as a star. Ray Price continues today to put

Buck Owens

Owens' first hit song "Act Naturally," released in 1963, was his biggest single. Fifteen consecutive number one records followed. *Photo courtesy of Jet Fellows.*

Ray Price
The Cherokee Cowboy

His timeless music, incredible voice, and innovative genius have yet to be equaled by any other singer in today's country music world. *Photo courtesy of Jet Fellows.*

country music in its proper place.

Hank William Thompson has been a major leader in western swing and honky-tonk music. The Waco-born legend has had songs charted for six decades. He is known for his monster hits "The Wild Side of Life," "Humpty Dumpty Heart," and "Six Pack to Go." Inducted into the Country Music Hall of Fame in 1989, he continues to build on his illustrious carrier. Hank Thompson was the first country star to perform in Las Vegas.

Hank Thompson

Ernest Tubb brought Hank Thompson to the Grand Ole Opry, but Thompson could foresee that he could not be innovative in experimenting with his fusion of western swing and honky-tonk by remaining in Nashville and moved back home to Texas. He is the only artist to have charted hit songs during six consecutive decades. *Photo courtesy of Jet Fellows.*

James Travis Reeves, born August 20, 1924, in Panola County, Texas, was first a broadcaster on the Louisiana Hayride before getting his opportunity to sing in the latter part of a 1952 show when Hank Williams failed to make an appearance. "Gentleman" Jim characterized the soft-edged Nashville sound with his rich, velvet voice. Some of the songs that identify Reeves are "Welcome to My World," "I Love you Because," "Billy Bayou" and the 1960 song of the year "He'll Have to Go." Inducted into the Country Music Hall of Fame in 1967, he died in a tragic plane crash on July 31, 1964.

Jim Reeves

Reeves was in the St. Louis Cardinals minor league organization until he suffered a leg injury that ended his career in baseball. The baritone singer scored his first number one song in 1953 with "Mexican Joe." "Four Walls," "He'll Have to Go," and "Welcome to my World" were some of his biggest hits. *Photo courtesy of Jet Fellows.*

One of country music's greatest songwriters and entertainers was born in Fort Worth on January 2, 1936. Roger Dean Miller could write a funny song and then make you cry with a sad one. His unique humor and musical skills entertained audiences who fell in love with his song compositions. In 1964 and 1965 he brought home eleven Grammy awards, which is still a record achievement. "Dang Me," "King of the Road" and "Chug-a-Lug" were songs that ignited his career. Stories told about Miller are priceless; he had the ability to create witty lines, and many are still told by the people who knew him. Just after he became a big star, those wits were reversed by a highway patrolman. Miller's close friend Grant Boatright recalled what happened one evening back in 1974 after a guest appearance on the "Tonight Show."

In a Volkswagen with Miller driving, Boatright up front, and Glen Campbell in the backseat, a highway patrolman pulled them over for speeding. The officer asked to see Miller's drivers license and Miller replied, "Can I shoot your gun?" "You're trying to be a wise guy," the officer snapped back and asked what he did for a living. By now Miller could see that he was not to be recognized and the officer could care less about who he was. "We play the Tonight Show every now and then," responded Miller, "but I see you work the nightshift and never get a chance to see it." The patrolman was getting fed up with all these smart-alec remarks and asked Miller to step out behind the car. As Miller walked behind his car, another officer recognized who he was, and after a little more conversation all three were allowed to leave. As Miller was driving away the patrolman turned on his loud speakers and sang, "Dang ya, dang ya, they oughta take a rope and hang ya."

Miller would close out his career earning a Tony Award for best musical score for the Broadway hit *Big River*. He died of lung cancer on October 25, 1992, and was inducted into the Country Music Hall of Fame in 1995.

When the topic of hardcore country singers comes up, George Jones is on top of the list. He entered the Country Music Hall of Fame in 1992. Born in the East Texas town of Saratoga on September 12, 1931, his first hit song was "Why Baby Why" in 1955. The traditional country songs that he has recorded epitomize the definition of country music. Jones won back-to-back single-of-the-year awards in 1980 and 1981 for the classic "He Stopped Loving Her Today." One of the finest country voices of all times, he no longer lives the drinking songs that he sings about.

Harry Choates (pronounced Shotes) was a music pioneer best known for updating and popularizing the Cajun classic "Jole Blon." Raised in Port Arthur, Texas, he was a master showman and an exceptional jazz guitarist, accordionist, steel guitarist, and fiddler who preferred to play on borrowed instruments. He worked in many clubs and dance halls throughout the state. Choates began drinking at an early age and suffered from chronic alcoholism. The troubled multi-instrumentalist made his first appearance at Dessau Hall with his band, The Melody Boys, on April 4, 1947. He often slept in the back of the hall after his wife left him. He was jailed in Austin for failure to pay child support and was declared dead in his cell three days later on July 17, 1951. How he actually died remains a mystery. Band members who had visited him claim that he died from police brutality, but in all probability he died from kidney deterioration. He was just twenty-eight years old. His headstone in Port Arthur cemetery reads "Parrain de la musique Cajun"—"The Godfather of Cajun Music."

Hank Harrison, music historian and leader of the award winning bluegrass band Tennessee Valley Authority, gave the following account of his interview with music pioneer Curly Williams to

George Jones performing at Shady Acres Resort in 1965

Jones is considered by many to be the greatest living country singer. Hank Williams and Lefty Frizzell were his idols. *Photo courtesy of Jet Fellows.*

preserve and document his amazing career. "Never the main star, Curly was a valuable asset to every band he joined. He played with dozens of Texas bands including The Texas Tune Wranglers, Jimmy Revard and the Oklahoma Playboys, The Three E's, and The Texas Tumbleweeds, which became the beginning of the Texas Top Hands. Known as a guitarist foremost, he also excelled on bass, fiddle, and banjo. Before settling down with these bands, he played medicine

The Tune Wranglers

The Tune Wranglers were one of the earliest western swing bands in San Antonio, led by Tom Dickey and Edwin "Buster" Coward. Dickey left the group to form his own band, Tom Dickey and the Showboys. Left to right, standing: Joe "Red Brown" Barnes, Eddie Whitley (pianist holding fiddle), and Charlie Gregg (upright bass) Seated: Tom Dickey (fiddle), Curley Williams (guitar), and Edwin "Buster" Coward (guitar). *Photo courtesy of Curley Williams.*

The Three E's Appearing nightly at the Monte Carlo Inn
San Antonio, Texas (1934)

Left to right: Lonnie "Happy" Williams, Charlie "Easy" Kowalie, and Curly Williams. The sign on the stage read, "The management is not responsible for any copyright music played or sung on these premises." *Photo courtesy of Curly Williams.*

shows, midnight Mexican dances, and even sang with blues legend Jelly Roll Morton in a Texas dance hall. He survived stints as a bull rider and even a gunfight with members of the infamous Dalton Gang on the streets of Oklahoma. Curly was involved in several historic recording sessions, including Ernest Tubb's first. 'I introduced Ernest to Eli Oberstein,' Curly remembers. The sessions were conducted by legendary record producer Oberstein, who had produced Bill Monroe's first record just six months earlier. The engineer on the session was Fred Lynch who had engineered the historic 1927 Bristol, Tennessee sessions, which resulted in Jimmie Rodgers and The Carter Family's first recordings. Curly was an important figure in the establishment of country music in Texas."

As country music experienced a country-politician era in the 1960s and 1970s with plain vanilla overproduced material, several artists were creating something a lot different in Texas. The progressive country movement which began in the early 1970s received little airplay on commercial radio and no attention at all from record labels in Nashville. For the first time there was a mix of cowboys, rednecks, and peace loving hippies enjoying this music in bars and dance halls across the state. Willie Nelson saw this developing at his performances at an old National Guard armory known as the Armadillo World Headquarters in Austin beginning in 1972. The Armadillo opened in 1970 and was managed by Eddie Wilson, Mike Tolleson, and Jim Franklin. Before closing on New Years Day 1981, it featured the top "progressive" country acts of the day. Austin, at that time, had a population of 250,000. It was not difficult to get around the town, especially when you compare what the work force traffic is like today. These were peaceful times, and a new genre of music spoke of those topics.

Austin venues hosted the likes of Michael Murphy, B.W. Stevenson, Steve Fromholtz, Ray Wylie Hubbard, Jerry Jeff Walker, Gary P. Nunn, The Lost Gonzos, Rusty Wier, and Asleep at the Wheel. Out west there was the Flying Burrito Brothers, Gram Parsons, Linda Ronstadt, Chris Hillman, Commander Cody, New Riders of the Purple Sage, and Emmylou Harris playing their brand of country/rock with some twang mixed in. Besides the Armadillo, where Commander Cody and his Lost Planet Airmen became the house band, there was the Skyline Club, Soap Creek Saloon, Castle Creek Saloon, the Broken Spoke, and the Texas Opry House to showcase these artists. The progressive country movement has never disappeared. Some of those venues may be long gone, but many of the artists who helped pioneer the movement are still around and staying as busy as ever.

In 1971 Willie Nelson decided to leave Nashville and return to Texas. His home in music city had burned down, and he wanted to make a living performing in dance halls in addition to his income from song royalties. He convinced Waylon Jennings to come down to experience what was developing at the Armadillo World Headquarters where new fan support was packing the venue. The timing just seemed right. Once word reached other artists that the Armadillo World Headquarters was attracting large crowds, Willie was contacted by Whispering Bill Anderson, who wanted to get in on the action. "Hell, they drink beer louder than you can sing in Texas," replied Willie. When Willie and Waylon recorded such duets as "Good Hearted Woman" and "Mamas Don't Let your Babies Grow Up to Be Cowboys," music critics labeled them "outlaws," as they totally ignored the Nashville establishment.

Willie Nelson was born in Abbott on April 29, 1933. He first gained notice as a songwriter after Faron Young recorded his song "Hello Walls." Patsy Cline followed with "Crazy" and then Ray Price's version of "Nightlife" established Willie as one of the top songwriters in country music. Willie first started playing in dance halls while in his teens, and the halls have supported his never tiring touring schedule through the years. After his 1975 debut on Columbia records, *Red Headed Stranger*, followed by *Wanted: The Outlaws* and *Stardust* albums, he had become country music's biggest star. His album collaboration *Wanted: The Outlaws*, with Jennings, Jesse Colter, and Tompall Glaser, became country music's first certified platinum record. He continues to be one of contemporary music's most beloved and active performers in the world. He is the driving force that maintains the tradition of country music. Willie was honored in 1993 when he entered the Country Music Hall of Fame.

Born on June 15, 1937, in Littlefield, Texas, Waylon Jennings first earned his reputation and success beginning in 1965 at RCA Records with Chet Atkins as his producer. He had already scored top tens on the charts before he and Willie released their *Outlaw* album. He played bass for Buddy Holly, giving up his seat to the Big Bopper (Jiles Perry Richardson) on the Iowa plane crash that also killed Holly

Willie Nelson, The Red Headed Stranger

Willie Nelson performing at Floore Country Store, 1969. Notice the pristine condition of Willie's guitar that he nicknamed "Trigger." "With hair as long as the generosity and talent as big as the heart, there is also a compassion that appears to be endless. Willie is a giant among men who lives inside a quite down to earth understanding." Leon Russell. *Photo courtesy of Steve Laughlin.*

and Ritchie Valens in 1959. Waylon joined the Country Music Hall of Fame in 2001. He died from diabetes-related illness on February 13, 2002.

The Jacksboro Highway, northwest of Fort Worth, became a breeding ground for many great Texas acts. The roadhouses along what was once the main artery to the West were places where Bruce Channel and Delbert McClinton first started their careers. Channel scored a huge hit in 1962 with "Hey Baby" that went to number one on the pop charts. McClinton played harmonica on the record and has built a career as one of the best R&B artists today. "Hey Baby" took them to England where a four-piece band known as the Beatles opened a show for them. The harmonica licks in the Beatles' song "Love Me Do" were inspired by McClinton.

West Texans Buddy Holly and Roy Orbison had an astounding effect on the world with their rock and roll and rockabilly music. The ·Beatles took their name from a version of Holly's band—The Crickets. The Fab Four polished their sound after being schooled by other Texans as well. When Doug Sahm and Augie Meyers toured England as the Sir Douglas Quintet following their hit "She's About a Mover," the Beatles shared the billing and were mesmerized by the sound coming out of Augie's vox organ. Within a couple of months there were two hundred vox organs for sale in music stores through-out England. Sahm once played steel guitar on Hank Williams' lap as an eleven-year-old music protégé when Williams performed at the Barn in San Antonio. The date also marked Hank's twenty-ninth birthday. Douglas Wayne Sahm would later take his country and blues influences and mix it with conjunto and rock to form a "South Texas/Westside San Antonio sound." Buck Owens' hit "Act Naturally" was covered by the Beatles and again shows the enormous impact that Texans have made on music around the world.

The early 1980s brought the "Urban Cowboy" era to Texas. It was a movement that took part of the roots away from country music. The 1980 Paramount movie *Urban Cowboy*, starring John Travolta, was filmed at Gilley's nightclub in Pasadena, Texas. The nightclub was a joint venture with Mickey Gilley and Sherwood Cryer and was famous long before the movie was seen on theaters across America. Located at 4500 Spencer Highway, it opened in 1971, closed in 1989, and burned down in 1990. It was billed as the world's largest honky-tonk and became the home of Gilley's band six nights a week. It had already hosted the likes of Merle Haggard, Roy Orbison, Mel Tillis, Hank Snow, Willie Nelson, Loretta Lynn, George Jones, Kitty Wells, and Faron Young. The late Houston pop critic Bob Claypool wrote, "It was quite simply, the most Texan of them all, the biggest, brawlingest, loudest, danceingest, craziest joint of its kind ever."

Country music saw an incline in popularity in the late 1980s and early 1990s in what is referred to as the new country and new traditionalist period. George Strait, born May 18, 1952, in Pearsall, came out of the chutes in the early 1980s and has been a proponent in keeping country music traditional. His straight-ahead country has won him many awards, and he has become one of the biggest stars in the business.

The new country and pop-oriented sound that blanketed America during the late 1990s and into the 2000s created a desire by fans for the return of roots country. In an article written by Jim Beal Jr., music critic for the *San Antonio Express-News*:

> If you haven't yet you'll soon hear the phrase "It's not your father's country music," or words to that effect. It all depends upon who your daddy is and what his musical tastes are, but there is yet another rogue country music breeze blowing across the land. Known as alt-country, alternative country or even "y'allternative," the music is experiencing, if not a huge boom, at least a respectable boomlet. Fans say it's largely a reaction to the sterility, homogenization and cookie-cutter approach to country music engendered by the Nashville establishment and commercial Top 40 country radio.

Trying to define alternative country music is a difficult task, but it can be best described as a type of sound that is too country for Top 40 country radio and just a little too twangy for rock and roll.

There are dance halls and musicians who may have been overlooked in this book, but I have tried to chronicle the journey Texas dance halls and country music has made over the years.

There are more Texans represented in the Country Music Hall of Fame than any other state. Each has made an enormous impact on the music, and many owe their success to the halls where they first started their careers. Each dance hall represented has a history of its own. Explore these unique venues and with it a wonderful excursion through the beautiful state of Texas. As the Texas Music Office states, "You can't hear American music without hearing Texas."

Slim Willet in the KRBC-TV Studio with
The Hired Hands and The Starlight Sisters

Born near Dublin, Texas, Willet is best remembered for his composition "Don't Let the Stars Get in Your Eyes," which was a number one hit song for him in 1952. Pop crooner Perry Como made it a top song a year later. Willet was on the Louisiana Hayride from 1951-1955 and also appeared on the Grand Ole Opry. *Photo courtesy of KRBC-TV.*

Airway Pavilion

Round Top, Texas ~ Fayette County

Airway Pavilion was moved from Wesley to Round Top around 1997. The hall used to sit on the northern Austin and Washington County line. Wooden braces held the propped windows open, hence the name Airway Pavilion. Built in the 1930s, locals would say they had danced in two counties in one evening.

Airway Pavilion is located next to The Antique Depot in Round Top on State Highway 237 and is now used to store antiques. Round Top is located eighteen miles north of La Grange.

Photo courtesy of Judy Cathey-Treviño

Albert Dance Hall

Albert, Texas ~ Gillespie County

Some of the first residents in the Albert area were George Cauley and Ben White Sr. Mr. Fritz Wilke purchased this land for cattle grazing from a man named Elmeier. Years later Elmeier was killed in a robbery.

Originally known as Martinsburg, it was changed in 1892 when a new post office was established by the infamous Albert Luckenbach, who had set up residence there after having sold the store and post office in Luckenbach, Texas, named in his honor.

The hall was built in 1922 by Max Beckman and featured German brass bands rotating between Luckenbach, Hye, and Weinheimer dance halls.

Lyndon Baines Johnson attended the Williams Creek school district at the small schoolhouse located next to the hall in 1920-1921. The old schoolhouse now functions as the community center, and the dance hall is used for storing feed.

Albert is located sixteen miles southeast of Fredericksburg on Farm Road 1623.

Photo courtesy of Judy Cathey-Treviño

American Legion Hall

Sealy, Texas ~ Austin County

The American Legion Hall in Sealy has been used for community functions, dances, and at one time as a skating rink. The hall was built around 1934.

The American Legion Hall in Sealy is located at 1630 Meyer St. on State Highway 36 at Interstate Highway 10 in Austin County west of Houston (409-885-7708).

Photo courtesy of Judy Cathey-Treviño

Anhalt Hall

Anhalt, Texas ~ Comal County

Anhalt is a German word meaning "stopping place." It was founded by German settlers in 1859. First known as Krauss Settlement, Anhalt Hall has been a meeting place for the Germania Farmer Verein (German Farmer Association) since 1875. It was formed in 1871 as a stock raiser's association for the protection of livestock from rustlers and Indians. After the Civil War, returning cowboys helped themselves to horses and cattle to round up and sell. The German colonists in south central Texas came up with a plan to prevent the theft of their livestock. The ranchers branded their cattle with the association brand, **G**, along with their own to help alert citizens and law enforcement officers of rustling. The program proved successful, and in 1875 the association revised its by-laws and it became a fraternal order for the preservation of the German language and culture in Texas.

Photo courtesy of Judy Cathey-Treviño

Interior view of Anhalt Hall
Photo courtesy of Judy Cathey-Treviño

The association maintains a benevolent fund that provides death benefits for its members. A ceremony is held at monthly meetings the first Sunday of the month and a resolution is sent to the family of the member who passed away, along with a death benefit of $500. The original purpose of the organization began to transform as members became involved in studying methods for improvement of livestock, agriculture, and horticulture. In 1877 the Verein obtained seeds from the Agriculture Department in Washington, D.C. A master farmer planted the seeds and then distributed crops to members after harvest time. The original 45 members now number around 600. The presence of Indians and unscrupulous highwaymen helped develop a strong organization that was invaluable to the community. The location was used as an overnight stop for people traveling from New Braunfels to Boerne, a four-day trip by wagon.

The association maintains a library consisting of around 500 volumes of works by Shakespeare and other classic literature, all in German. These books are on permanent loan to the Institute of Texan Cultures in San Antonio. An interesting fact is that the present treasurer of the Verein is only the sixth since the start of the organization. Harvey Schaefer, a member of the Verein, stated that his dad was the club's treasurer for many years and translated minutes of meetings from German to English.

In May of 1877 the Verein held a picnic that was so successful it was decided to have exhibits of field and garden products and live-stock in conjunction with the celebration of a planting festival, Oktoberfest, in the fall. Members invite the public to celebrate Mayfest, Summerfest, and Oktoberfest as they have since 1877. The traditional food of pot roast, peas, potato salad, and sauerkraut is served, and the festivities continue with a dance. In 1936 the club celebrated the centennial of Texas with a large gathering. Unfortunately, no documentation has been found.

Founding fathers of Anhalt
Photo courtesy of Germania Farmer Verein

Limestone surrounds the foundation of the original hall that was built in 1875. In 1908 a larger portion with a 6,000-square-foot oak dance floor and pier and beam construction was added. The rafters bow across the ceiling of the hall, and steel rods run below the rafters to help brace the structure together. Rhett Stuman replaced all the louvers and screens above the hall, beer garden, and kitchen areas. With high ceilings and large fans built at each end of the hall, the air current it creates provides for great ventilation. The bandstand was added to the dance hall sometime after 1908. Rhett painted the

122nd Annual May Fest celebration, Anhalt Hall
Photo courtesy of Germania Farmer Verein

lettering on the outside that reads **ANHALT 1908.** Signs in the hall reflect what the Verein was trying to maintain to show proper respect to all.

"NO SHORTS-PEDAL PUSHERS-T-SHIRTS OR BLUE JEANS ALLOWED ON THE DANCE FLOOR"

"INDECENT-UNCOMMONLY-DANCING-IN-
THIS-HALL-IS-STRICTLY-PROHIBITED"
THE VEREIN

Up until the early eighties hats were not to be worn on the dance floor. In 1996 the association purchased fifteen acres that adjoined the hall and original ten acres. Profits from the three yearly celebrations are used to help preserve the hall. In recent years a new roof was added, the dance floor was refurbished, and a porch on the east side of the hall was built.

In October 1997, with picture perfect weather and *The Dallas Morning News* at the hall to do a special feature story on historic Texas dance halls, Oktoberfest was celebrated. The Bohemian Dutchmen played the traditional old-time polka and waltz music in the afternoon. Country music by the Geronimo Band, with the sun going down and a slight chill in the air, rounded out the rest of the evening. Wilton Stuebing, president of the Verein, and his son Ronnie celebrated their fiftieth and twenty-fifth wedding anniversaries together with their wives, family, and friends in March of 1998. The double anniversary celebration was highlighted with the traditional Grand March.

Benches surround the dance floor as is common in these old

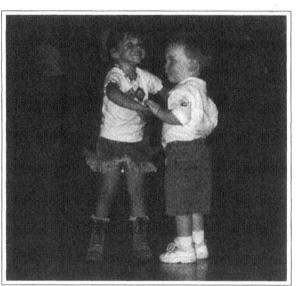

Young dancers at Anhalt Hall.
Photo courtesy of Judy Cathey-Treviño

Johnny Rodriguez
Anhalt Hall (July 25, 1998)
Photo courtesy of Judy Cathey-Treviño

halls. There is a picture of the Wm. Specht Spring Branch Band that was formed in 1880 and played at Anhalt. They were a six-piece all brass band, the first in Comal County. George Strait performed at Anhalt Hall for an FFA dance for Smithson Valley High School in 1978. Lately, Gary P. Nunn, Clay Blaker, Chris Wall, Geronimo Treviño, Johnny Rodriguez, and Jerry Jeff Walker have kept dancers waltzing and two stepping on an old floor that lets you glide as if you are dancing on glass. This is a great haven for all the kids who slide around in their socks before the show and during breaks at dances.

New members are nominated and their credentials are discussed at monthly meetings. If elected they promise to abide by the constitution and by-laws of the Germania Farmer Verein. The movie *All the Pretty Horses*, starring Matt Damon and Penelope Cruz and directed by Billy Bob Thorton, had a love scene filmed at the historical dance hall. The Germania Farmer Verein is a nonprofit organization benefiting the preservation of the German heritage and supporting local agriculture.

Anhalt Hall is in Comal County and is located on Anhalt Road, one mile off Highway 46, twenty-eight miles west of New Braunfels. Anhalt Road is 4.5 miles west of U.S. Highway 281.

Arkey Blue's Silver Dollar Bar

Bandera, Texas ~ Bandera County

Fifty miles northwest of San Antonio is a charming little town, set in a bend of the Medina River and surrounded by limestone hills that are covered with oak, cedar, and bigtooth maple. Cypress trees tower along the Medina River, and the road winds through some of the most scenic parts of the Texas hill country. Welcome to Bandera, Texas. Proclaimed "The cowboy capital of the world" due to its western heritage, architecture, and thirteen dude ranches in the area, Bandera caters to this way of life.

Photo courtesy of Judy Cathey-Treviño

Interior view of Arkey Blue's Silver Dollar
Photo courtesy of Judy Cathey-Treviño

Tonkawa Indians referred to this area as "Valley of Paints." Various colorful clays provided face paint for medicine men. In the late 1600s Lipan Apache and later Comanche drove them out of the valley. These Indians used the color pigment from the clays as war paint in their battles with Spanish soldiers attempting to explore Texas. Soldiers looking for gold and friars searching for souls were also attacked by the Comanche. Bandera Pass, a natural ambush point, offered the only easily traveled path to the Edwards Plateau and points west. In 1841 forty Texas Rangers fought more than 200 Comanches in a battle eventually won by the rangers.

Bandera was originally a cypress shingle camp. In 1854 a band of Mormon disciples built a mill race and began milling grains. By 1855 the town had been surveyed and a group of Polish settlers had moved in, founding the second oldest Polish community in the United States. Cypress trees provided dwellings and jobs for the community after the Civil War.

Bandera also prospered with the rebirth of the cattle industry, and Bandera found itself on one of the feeder routes of the Chisholm Trail cattle drives. For twenty years, thousands of Texas longhorns were driven up the Medina River from south Texas, headed for Abilene, Kansas, and the Union Pacific railroad. Many a cowboy spent his wages in Bandera for a night on the town. Bandera remained a center of ranching activity after the decline of the cattle industry with cowboys working throughout the county.

As the years passed, rodeo took over as a way of life for the local cowboys. Seven Bandera County men have taken national and world championships. Six-time all around cowboy Larry Mahan lived close by in Camp Verde before moving to Cripple Creek, Colorado, to train horses.

Main Street is full of characters that keep the cowboy tradition alive, and country music has always taken center stage in this western town. For years people could enjoy the big band music of Tommy Dorsey, the western swing of Bob Wills, and other country legends at the Silver Spur. It burned down in the late fifties.

People still supported the Cabaret through the years, but 1968 gave birth to a new little honky-tonk, Arkey Blue's Silver Dollar Bar. What you get at Arkey's is straight up traditional country music. Each Friday and Saturday night Arkey and his band play songs he has written about cheatin', honky-tonkin', and about dogs and slow horses. As you enter through the front door and walk down a flight of stairs, you find yourself ankle deep in sawdust and into a time zone of days gone by. Arkey Blue and the Silver Dollar Bar is the real thing.

Ernest Tubb once played there as well as many other noted singers throughout the years. Parts of Peter Fonda's movie *Race With the Devil* have footage of the Silver Dollar Bar in it. Arkey's songs have been used in *Texas Chainsaw Massacre* ("Daddy's Sick Again"), and his "Misty Hours of Daylight" can be heard in *Race with the Devil*. The jukebox is filled with country music by Hank Williams, Marty Robbins, and of course, Arkey himself. Posters on the walls take you back in time when country music was country music.

Arkey has performed for many famous people ranging from movie stars to sports figures. His CD *The Best of Arkey Blue* has sold well in Europe. In 1990 *Texas Highways Magazine* named Arkey Blue's Silver Dollar Bar one of the top three honky-tonks in Texas. Popular Texas singer/songwriter Robert Earl Keen resides in Bandera. Robert made a tape of seven songs written by Arkey that have the word "Bandera" in the lyrics to take with him when traveling on the road.

Arkey Blue and Judy Parker
Photo courtesy of Greg Holland

The Silver Dollar Bar is located at 308 Main Street in Bandera, Texas, in east central Bandera County (830-796-8826). Bandera is located on State Highway 16, fifty miles northwest of San Antonio.

Bellville Turnverein Pavilion

Bellville, Texas ~ Austin County

In the nineteenth century, two organizations, the Bellville Social Club and the Bellville Turnverein Gut Heil (meaning good health in German), sponsored community-wide social activities. The Social Club purchased property from Herman Miller in 1883 and planned construction of a pavilion. The Bellville Turnverein, founded in 1885, built an opera house in 1889, which became the center of the town's social activities.

Photo courtesy of Judy Cathey-Treviño

In 1895 the Turnverein purchased the Social Club's property and hired local contractor Joachim Hintz to build the pavilion, which was completed in 1897. The twelve-sided structure required extra long lumber, which was shipped directly from the mills.

The city of Bellville purchased the property and pavilion in 1937 and sponsored a competition among Texas A&M students to redesign the park. The winning design, along with a grant from the Federal Works Progress Administration, enabled the city to build new facilities and update the pavilion with modern amenities. It continues to serve as a focal point for many community gatherings.

Bellville is located at the junction of State Highways 36 and 159 in central Austin County. The hall is located just past the intersection of Farm Roads 159 and 529 in Bellville.

Big John's Hangin' Tree Saloon

Bracken, Texas ~ Comal County

Just northeast of San Antonio, two blocks from the Bexar County line, in Comal County, is the small community of Bracken. Settled in 1849

Trail riders gathering up to head out to the San Antonio Livestock Show and Rodeo after an evening at the Hangin' Tree Saloon.
Photo courtesy of Judy Cathey-Treviño

by William Bracken, known for having lost three fingers when Texas rebels overpowered a Mexican fort on the Nueces River. Bracken was the first owner of the lands known as the Vicenti Micheli League. These lands were once owned by the state of Texas, and the grant was signed by P.H. Bell, governor of Texas. The property totaled 1,114 acres and was located in the counties of Comal and Bexar by Cibolo Creek where the San Antonio and Nacogdoches Roads crossed.

In June of 1853, Mary, Robert, and Eliza Schneider became owners of this property through court proceedings as legal heirs of William

Big John Oaks and Geronimo in front of the Hangin' Tree Saloon.
Photo courtesy of Judy Cathey-Treviño

Bracken as was stated in his last will and testament. On November 16, 1880, the International and Great Northern Railroad bought 54.7 acres of this land for a railroad right-of-way. On December 31, 1890, J.S. Barnes and J.S. Wetmore merged with the New York and Texas Land Company Limited. The name of the township of Davenport was changed to Bracken on July 14, 1899.

Between 1880 and 1890 the railroad was built and started the building of a typical western community. The railroad constructed a depot and employed a ticket agent at that time. A post office with daily mail routes was set up and two large general merchandise stores were built by Mr. Fromme and by Mr. Fenske, with Fromme's Store housing a hotel on the second story. At one time a saloon and dance hall were located next to each store.

Bracken is on the opposite side of the railroad tracks from Cibolo Creek Country Club/Luxello Hall. The town is famous for two things: Bracken Cave and Big John's Hangin' Tree Saloon.

Bracken Cave has one of the largest concentrations of mammals

An evening with Johnny Duncan at the Hangin' Tree. Duncan has recorded number one songs such as "Thinkin' of a Rendezvous," "Sweet Country Woman," "Stranger," "It Couldn't Have Been Any Better," and "She Can Put Her Shoes Under My Bed Anytime." *Photo courtesy of Judy Cathey-Treviño*

in the world. Biologists estimate 20 million Mexican freetailed bats inhabit the cave with almost all being pregnant females carrying a single pup. When fall approaches, the births multiply the colony to almost twice the original population. Biologists "guesstimate" that before the bats leave in the fall, they will have deposited around eighty tons of bat guano. The prized and rich fertilizer was once a top export for Texas during the first quarter of the twentieth century.

Big John's Hangin' Tree Saloon was once a two-lane, nine-pin bowling alley built in 1915. It has been enlarged to twice its original size. The bowling alley was remodeled in 1956 and closed in 1978. A new bowling alley was built across the street.

In 1989 Big John Oaks turned the old bowling alley into a roadhouse honky-tonk in typical Texas fashion. The bar is made from wood that was once the lanes of the bowling alley. The bandstand is located where the bowling pins used to be placed. Their slogan is "Now that you've found Luckenbach, where the heck is Bracken."

Lawyers, businessmen, and just plain "good ole boys" enjoy getting away from hectic work schedules to enjoy the atmosphere of

"The Tree." Actor Tommy Lee Jones has slipped into Big John's after playing polo at the polo fields close by. In fact he still owes Big John for one beer he never paid for. The opening of Retama Park Race-track, one and one half miles away, has brought in horse jockeys and other personnel to come and relax after working at the track.

In the fall of 1996, a radio programmer from Denmark visited her first honky-tonk and fell in love with The Hangin' Tree. The Alamo Kountry Kicker Trail Riders host a dance each February to help kick off the San Antonio Livestock Show and Rodeo. The trail riders camp out at different spots on their way to the rodeo grounds, and this is one of their designated stops.

Several characters help patronize and add color to Big John's place. Mayor Sam Bauder of nearby Cibolo, Texas, is a regular cus-tomer. One weekend, after my band finished a Friday and Saturday performance, I noticed the same guy sitting on the same barstool he had occupied the night before. As we were packing our equipment up, he told Big John, "Now that's a much better band tonight than the one from the night before." I bring that up to Big John every now and then, and we always get a big laugh out of it.

The Hangin' Tree Saloon can hold about 175 people inside, and patrons can enjoy the outdoor patio in the back of the hall if it gets too crowded inside. There is a kitchen by the patio called Planet Bracken that serves some great barbecue, nachos, and hamburgers. Local bands play every Friday and Saturday with some occasional Sunday shows. Sonny Throckmorton, Freddie Powers, Johnny Duncan, Augie Meyers, Johnny Bush, Gary P. Nunn, and Johnny Rodriguez have all entertained at The Hangin' Tree. At times it's been so crowded that if a dog were to slip in under the swinging doors, it would only be able to wag its tail up and down.

> *There's a place down the road called the Hangin' Tree,*
> *Where I can go to have a beer and just be me.*
> *Ain't no fancy mirror balls, ain't no painted bathroom walls,*
> *It's just what a Texas honky-tonk should be.*
> From the "Hangin' Tree Song" written by Jeff Simonson

From San Antonio take Nacogdoches Road north from Loop 1604 about two miles and right after you cross Cibolo Creek and the rail-road tracks take the first right (on Bracken Road) and you are in

Bracken. Go down that road to 2nd Street and take a left and "The Tree" is on your right. 18424 2nd Street, 210-651-5812. Open every day. Music Friday, Saturday, and Sunday.

Bleiblerville SPJST Dance Hall

Bleiblerville, Texas ~ Austin County

This community was named after an early general store proprietor by the name of Robert Bleiber. When I first tried to pronounce Bleiblerville (*Bly-blur-ville*) one might have thought I had been sipping on a few glasses of fine wine. The Czech hall was built in 1915 and remodeled in 1955. Many of these dance halls and community centers have added metal siding to the outside walls to keep the draft out and paneling on the inside interior. Air conditioners have been installed, and modern conveniences have given these old buildings a much newer look. This is evident in Bleiblerville.

Nelsonville SPJST merged with Bleiblerville SPJST, and meetings are held now in Bleiblerville. (The SPJST, Slavic Benevolent

Photo courtesy of Judy Cathey-Treviño

Order of the State of Texas Society, is one of the oldest Czech-American organizations in the United States.) The hall remains an important part of the community with many social events and dances being held at there. Annual fish fries on the third Sunday of May and October continue to serve the public every year.

Bleiblerville is located on Farm Road 2502, four miles northeast of Industry in northwest Austin County. Coming from Nelsonville take 2503 north three miles and the hall is on the right, just across the road from the post office.

Blumenthal Dance Hall

Blumenthal, Texas ~ Gillespie County

Around the mid-1850s, the governor of Texas granted land to Charles Bullard in the vicinity of Blumenthal. The area containing the type of soil that produced colorful displays of wildflowers led to the naming of the community as Blumenthal, a German word meaning blooming valley.

Photo courtesy of Marilyn Schulz

Two brothers, Max and Eugene Hohenberger, from nearby Grapetown are actually recognized as having settled the town of Blumenthal. They ran a saloon in a two-story building and soon saw the need for a larger one that was built fifty feet to the east. The new Blumenthal dance hall was built around 1900 and hosted many dances. In 1908 Max and Eugene's parents, Ferdenand and Caroline, celebrated their fiftieth wedding anniversary at the hall. Virginia and Ed Tinkle converted the old hall into a bed and breakfast established in 1995. The land with the hall, two-story saloon, and gingerbread farmhouse was sold to John and Marilyn Schulz in 1999. They continue to maintain this piece of Texas treasure as a bed and breakfast facility.

Blumenthal is located seven miles east of Fredericksburg and five miles west of Stonewall on U.S. Highway 290.

Left to right: John Kunz, Max and Eugene Hohenberger standing in front of the two saloons in Blumenthal. The quarts of whiskey that the men are holding are to celebrate the first bale of cotton that came off the cotton gin. Photo circa 1916. *Photo courtesy of Marilyn Schulz and Leonard Hohenberger.*

Braun Hall

Helotes, Texas ~ Bexar County

The Texas Hill Country Baseball League hosted teams from several towns in central Texas. Teams from Boerne, Comfort, Fredericksburg, Hondo, D'Hanis, and Helotes would travel each Sunday to compete against each other during the summer months. I played for the Klassing Oilers and Helotes Hawks the last two years the league was in existence, which ended in 1971. Our home field was next to Braun Hall in Helotes, Texas. Games always started at 1:00 P.M. Sunday, and after the game was over we would take off our baseball cleats, put on our tennis shoes, and go into the hall. With warm summer breezes entering through propped-opened windows, we would wind down after our games, drinking a few beers, rehashing the game, and listening to country music on the jukebox.

Photo courtesy of Judy Cathey-Treviño

Fred Spears was one of my teammates when I played for Helotes. His brother Bea has played bass for Willie Nelson for many years. In Fredericksburg, which had two teams the last year of the league, home games were played next to Pat's Hall. After our games against Fredericksburg teams, we would go to Pat's and do exactly the same things we did at Braun Hall.

Built in 1893, Braun Hall still has weekly dances every Saturday night and Sunday afternoon. They rotate a few local bands from the area and have some serious dancers scootin' across a beautiful 35 x 70 foot oak floor. Its capacity is around 500. Braun Hall was renovated in 1949 and enclosed in 1995, and air conditioning was added then. It is run by the Fraternal Hermann Sons organization and managed by Evelyn Carolan, who is part of the Braun family. It caters to an older crowd. Evelyn stated that their motto is "If you're dancin', you're not dying."

Braun Hall is located close to Helotes, Texas, at 9721 Braun Road, in northwest Bexar County (210-688-9241). From Loop 1604 going westbound just past State Highway 16, take a left on Braun Road and the hall is less than one half mile on the left. Dances every Saturday night and Sunday afternoon.

Broken Spoke

Austin, Texas ~ Travis County

The Broken Spoke in Austin was built to look like an old vintage dance hall. James White, its proprietor, enjoyed listening to an old radio show called "Broken Arrow" and liked wagon wheels, so he combined these two loves to create the Broken Spoke. The Spoke was once surrounded by the Al Ehrlich Lumberyard, before James dismantled it to make room for his dance hall.

The Broken Spoke opened on November 10, 1964, and has been an Austin tradition, focusing on original and classic country music. Videos of Asleep at the Wheel, Chris Wall, and movies *Honeysuckle Rose* with Willie Nelson, *Wild Texas Wind* with Dolly Parton, and

Photo courtesy of Judy Cathey-Treviño

Dance Across Texas, as well as the BBC documentary *Texas Saturday Night*, have all been filmed at the Spoke and show what a true Texas honky-tonk is.

The Texas State Legislature has given the venue a citation commending it for its services, and *Texas Highways Magazine* named it "Best Honky-Tonk In Texas" in 1990.

Hank Thompson, Ernest Tubb, Willie Nelson (Willie was paid $800 to play there in 1968), George Strait, Tex Ritter, Roy Acuff, Grandpa Jones, and Bob Wills have all played the Spoke. When Bob Wills played, he never sang one song, just played fiddle and hollered, "Take it away, Leon." Besides these great legends that have entered the dance hall, the Queen of England's entourage have enjoyed the best of country music at the Spoke.

The bands playing there now that keep the tradition alive are Jerry Jeff Walker, Gary P. Nunn, Alvin Crow, Chris Wall, The Geezinslaw Brothers, Cornell Hurd, Don Walser, Dale Watson, and the Derailers.

Called the "last of the true Texas dance halls," it has a seating capacity of 660. The low ceiling keeps the sound right on top of the dance floor. A room located to the left of the hall houses some interesting memorabilia. Photos, hats, and even a half-smoked cigar belonging to Bob Wills are in what is called "The Tourist Trap Room."

Interior view of Broken Spoke.
Photo courtesy of Judy Cathey-Treviño

Coach Darrell Royal would sometimes have a spiritual pick-me-up party for his great University of Texas football teams at the Spoke. Occasionally Willie Nelson would help inspire the team through his music. This was yet another fine tactic used by Coach Royal.

The Broken Spoke is located at 3201 South Lamar Blvd. just north of Ben White Blvd. in Austin (512-442-6189).

Buckholts SPJST Lodge 15

Buckholts, Texas ~ Milam County

The town was named for John A. Buckholts after he donated land for the Gulf, Colorado and Sante Fe Railway in 1881. The SPJST (Slavic Benevolent Order of the State of Texas) was first organized in July of 1897. Two dance halls were in use before the hall that stands today was built. The first hall was dedicated on July 4, 1911, and was

Buckholts Dance Hall, 1915, destroyed by fire in 1936.
Photo courtesy of Mrs. Charlsie Svetlik

destroyed by a devastating storm in August of 1915. A second hall
was leveled by a fire in March of 1936. This did not faze the small
community as they constructed another hall four months later. On
June 7, 1936, the eight-sided structure was completed, and it has
served the area well through the years. It is still in use for wedding
receptions and reunions, and local Czech bands perform for club
dances the second Sunday of the month. Mrs. Charlsie Svetik, a
member of the lodge since 1947, has served as secretary to the organization since 1963. She recalls the beautiful arch-like ceiling that
characterized the interior of the building. When the modernization of
air conditioning was necessary, the ceiling was covered up and a new
one lowered to replace it. Before all these comforts, Charlsie remembers, "When we danced, whether it be cold or hot inside the hall, we
always had a good time."

On October 5, 1997, the SPJST celebrated their 100-year anniversary. The membership is 410 strong.

The Vrazel Polka Band leased the hall from 1957 to 1971 and
remains one of the longest running Czech bands to play in Texas,
originating in 1953. Brothers Anton, Lawrence, Albert, and Alfred
Vrazel have performed in most of these old halls throughout the

Buckholts Dance Hall, 2001.
Photo courtesy of Judy Cathey-Treviño

state. Radio station KTAE out of Taylor used to broadcast live shows from the hall in the early 1950s. Jimmy Heep, Hank Thompson, and Bob Wills were on some of those shows, which aired each Thursday evening. Other famous names that played the hall were Slim Whitman, Johnny Horton, Jim Reeves, Web Pierce, Billy Walker, Kitty Wells, and Little Jimmy Dickens.

Buckholts is located nine miles northwest of Cameron on Highway 36 in northwest Milam County.

Cabaret Cafe and Dance Hall

Bandera, Texas ~ Bandera County

The Bandera Cabaret opened its doors in 1936 as a small honky-tonk that catered to folks in nearby counties. Military trainees in San Antonio and Hondo helped popularize the Cabaret, and in the 1940s it was

Neon sign in front of the Cabaret.
Photo courtesy of Judy Cathey-Treviño

enlarged to its present size. The famous "hump" on the dance floor was caused by an uneven pour of concrete during the expansion. Past owners decided to leave it rather than make the effort to break it up and level it. It gives you a strange sensation as you dance over that portion of the 2,400-square-foot dance floor. The hall is over 10,000 square feet.

Located just east of Arkey Blue's Silver Dollar Bar in downtown Bandera, it has hosted country music's biggest stars over the years. Hank Williams, Loretta Lynn, Hank Thompson, Bob Wills, Jim Reeves, Ray Price, Willie Nelson, Ernest Tubb, Roger Miller, and Johnny Bush have all performed there. Doug Sahm once hosted a "live" radio show from the Cabaret, and Willie Nelson filmed a show for his "Outlaw Satellite Network" in 1990 with special guests Billy Joe Shaver and Johnny Bush.

George Chambers, who has played many of these halls since the late 1950s, recalls seeing Roger Miller opening a show for Ray Price in the early sixties. Ray's big song at the time was "Heartaches By the Number." Before the show began, Roger was going around the crowd holding a French horn with a tricycle horn attached to it and making honking noises.

Larry Nolen played at the Cabaret for seventeen years and began his music career there. He had a big hit with a country version of "Rambling Rose." On February 14, 1998, we celebrated Valentines Day and Larry's birthday, taking turns sharing the stage. The day marked fifty years to the day that he first played there.

The dude ranches around Bandera bring in people who enjoy going to the Cabaret year after year. In the winter months, deer hunters enjoy going to hear country music and the traditions of the famous venue. The opening day of deer season is a huge weekend all over Bandera.

Ralph Mitchell owned the Cabaret for forty years, and it has been through several owners. The Bandera Cabaret was purchased in 1998 by Thurman Love, and a new tradition of country singer/songwriter is taking it into the new millennium. Now called Cabaret Cafe and Dance Hall, Thurman's booking policy has focused on new artists. No Nashville "hat acts" or Top 40 country singers will be performing there. Ray Wylie Hubbard, Darrell McCall, Dale Watson, Don Walser, The Derailers, The Hollisters, Hank Thompson, Guy Clark, Steve Earle, Gary P. Nunn, Asleep at the Wheel, The Time

Caesare Masse performing at the Cabaret.
Photo courtesy of Caesare Masse

Guy Clark at the Cabaret (April 8, 1999).
Photo courtesy of Judy Cathey-Treviño

Floyd Tillman performing at the age of 85 years young at the Cabaret.
Photo courtesy of Judy Cathey-Treviño

Warp Hands, and local hometown favorites Bruce and Charlie Robison are the refreshing type of performers playing there now. The traditional country music that the Cabaret is famous for continues through these artists. Robert Earl Keen played the grand re-opening October 10, 1998. The sign out front read "New roof—new food, same ole hump." Great food and great music in a great little town.

Take State Highway 16 west from San Antonio, fifty miles to Bandera, Texas. The Cabaret is at 801 Main Street (830-796-8166). Thurman Love, owner.

Smiley Whittley and his band with special guests,
Homer and Jethro (June 19, 1952) at the Cabaret.

Left to right: J. R. Chatwell, Cal Berry, Homer Haynes, Smiley, Jethro Burns, unknown,
Little David Frazier, and kneeling Peewee "Meatball" Maples. *Photo courtesy of Mrs.
J. R. Chatwell.*

Curly Williams and
Louise Grubert
Williams. Wedding
photo from the
Cabaret (December
18, 1947).
*Photo courtesy of
Curly Williams.*

Carmine Dance Hall

Carmine, Texas
Fayette/Washington County Line

This community was first known as Sylvan but was renamed Carmine in 1892 after the town's first postmaster, Newton Carmean. The railroad and U.S. Highway 290 became an important link between Houston and Austin. By 1964 Highway 290 was moved and bypassed Carmine, and the railroad line closed.

Carmine Dance Hall hosts an annual Christmas Fest and has been the site of various antique shows.

Carmine is located on U.S. Highway 290 at the Fayette-Washington County line. The Carmine Dance Hall is located off Spur 458 just north of Highway 290.

Photo courtesy of Judy Cathey-Treviño

Cat Spring Agricultural Society Hall

Cat Spring, Texas ~ Austin County

Cat Spring is a pioneer German settlement founded in 1832 by members of the Ambler, Kleberg, and Von Roeder families. First known as "Katzenquelle," the community was renamed Wildcat Spring after the first settlers saw numerous wildcats in the area. It was later shortened to Cat Spring. By 1850 Czech settlers made their way into Cat Spring, and as the area continued to grow, the need to learn agricultural methods was of major concern. The Landwirth Schaftlide Verein was organized in 1856 to help educate the people about agriculture and farming. The organization was later known as the Austin County Agricultural Society before becoming today's Cat Spring Agricultural Society.

Photo courtesy of Judy Cathey-Treviño

The first hall that was built in Cat Spring burned down in 1895. Joachin Hintz built a rectangular shaped hall shortly afterwards, which was named Turner Hall. It served the community until being torn down in 1958. The need for another pavilion to satisfy the growth of the community was decided on September 7, 1902. Hintz presented his plans to members and was given approval to begin construction immediately, and the twelve-sided Agricultural Society Hall was completed within five months. The hall sits on exterior piers made of brick that was hand pressed in nearby New Ulm, Texas. The center pole supporting the roof allowed more room to dance, and dancers always rotated counterclockwise around the pole. New improvements were made by 1931 when the bandstand was moved to the northwest side of the hall and a concrete column supporting twelve cone radials replaced the original center pole. In the 1950s a bar, restroom, and kitchen were added to the hall.

In the past, the beautiful structure has been the host of July 4th celebrations, Mai-Fest, harvest festivals, and Christmas and New Years Eve dances. The St. Bernard Electric Cooperative has their annual meetings at the hall. Weddings, anniversaries, antique shows, and the annual June Fest and Barbecue continue to make the Society Hall the centerpiece of Cat Spring.

To visit the Agricultural Society Hall go eleven miles northwest of Sealy on Farm Road 1094 and the hall is just past the crossroads.

Cestohowa Dance Hall

Cestohowa, Texas ~ Karnes County

Named after a city in Poland, Cestohowa (originally spelled Czestochowa) is located one mile west of Highway 123 in northern Karnes County. As Polish immigrants filtered into Panna Maria, Cestohowa and Kosciusko soon became new settlements for the growing number of new residents.

Ray Sczepanik used to sit by the stage and listen to his idols, The Texas Top Hands, perform at the hall when he was ten years old.

Photo courtesy of Judy Cathey-Treviño

Years later he would become their bandleader. Since 1945 The Texas Top Hands have been managed at one time or another by Easy Adams, Rusty Locke, Walt Klepas, and Ray Sczepanik. When Ray's mother passed away, she was buried at the cemetery located behind the hall.

From State Highway 123 in northern Karnes County, take Farm Road 3191 (right after Cibolo Creek) a mile west into Cestohowa.

Cherry Springs Dance Hall

Cherry Spring, Texas ~ Gillespie County

Cherry Springs Dance Hall was established by Herman Lehmann around 1890. Born on June 5, 1859, to German immigrants after they settled on land in Loyal Valley, he was captured by Mescalero

Photo courtesy of Judy Cathey-Treviño

Apaches when he was eleven years old. For the next nine years he lived with the Indians, gaining warrior status, and eventually joined the Comanches after killing an Apache medicine man in a drunken brawl. He lived the life of a hermit for a year before joining Comanche chief Quanah Parker. Parker was the son of Cynthia Ann Parker, who was captured by the Comanches in 1835. Quanah Parker's father, Nocoma, was the leader of the Kwahadi band, one of the fiercest of all Comanche tribes. Quanah Parker and his tribe adopted Lehmann and later talked him into returning to his former life and joining his mother, brothers, and sisters in Loyal Valley.

After being brought back from his captivity, he had a difficult time readjusting to Anglo life. On many occasions he would dress in Indian garb and scare children. Lehmann spent most of his time drinking, gambling, and fighting. Easy money was made at Cherry Springs Dance Hall, but he sold it after gaining a considerable amount of weight and loving whiskey too much. "My career has been rather checkered; I have lived as a savage and as a civilized man." When I mentioned these characteristics to David Zettner he responded, "What a nice combination to have as a club owner. You actually have

Cherry Springs Dance Hall sign.
Photo courtesy of Judy Cathey-Treviño

to possess those traits to be successful nowadays."

Wagon wheel chandeliers, custom made cedar tables, and a hand carved cypress bar accent the beautiful 1,400-square-foot wooden dance floor. It has a small twelve-foot-deep stage, and the entire hall is 11,000 square feet, with several rooms. There is also a rodeo arena in the back of the property.

Legends who have performed there read like the "History of Country Music." Hank Williams, Lefty Frizzell, Patsy Cline, Ernest Tubb, Asleep at the Wheel, Bob Wills, Faron Young, Ray Price, Willie Nelson, Buck Owens, Nat King Cole, Caesare Masse, George Jones, Adolph Hofner, Little Jimmy Dickens, Johnny Horton, and Marty Robbins all played there. At times Marty Robbins would perform on Saturday and Sunday.

On Sunday, October 9, 1955, the Louisiana Hayride Tour with Elvis Presley, Johnny Horton, Ferlin Huskey, and other cast members performed at Cherry Springs to an overflow crowd. Admission was $1.50. The poster advertising the Hayride Tour had Elvis's name spelled as Clovis Presley. He did not headline the show either. Five weeks later Sam Phillips sold the contract he had with Elvis on Sun Records to RCA for $35,000. Jayson Fritz, of KFAN Texas Rebel Radio in Fredericksburg, remembers his father bringing Elvis to their

Walter Kleypas and the Lone Star Band

Left to right: Smitty Highsmith (piano), J. R. Chatwell (fiddle), Dave Spencer (drums), Charlie Harris (guitar), Norman Jordan (steel guitar), and Walter Kleypas. Suits, hats, boots, and buckles were furnished by Lone Star Beer Company. *Photo courtesy of Junior Mitchan.*

home after visiting their family-owned radio station, KNAF. Jayson said Elvis was a polite young man and even picked up his little sister in a playful gesture. Fredericksburg has never quite been the same since. Old posters with signatures of all the big stars who played at Cherry Springs have disappeared over the years.

Cherry Springs has remained open, off and on, through the years. In 1994 D.C. Owens purchased the hall.

Cherry Springs Dance Hall is located in Northern Gillespie County on State Highway 87, eighteen miles north of Fredericksburg (830-997-0132).

Cibolo Creek Country Club/Luxello Hall

San Antonio, Texas ~ Bexar County

Luxello Hall once served as a general store/railroad depot/voting complex and as a gathering place for locals to meet. It is located on the Bexar/Comal County line just northeast of San Antonio. The Missouri-Pacific Railroad, which runs between Cibolo Creek and Bracken, Texas, at one time helped this community, known briefly as Landa, prosper. Named for Charles Lux, the hall was built around 1904. After having been dormant for several years, the hall re-opened in 1990 as Cibolo Creek Country Club.

Denny Johnson, with his longtime friends Linda and Tim Holt, refurbished the hall and turned it into a great Texas roadhouse

Photo courtesy of Judy Cathey-Treviño

Interior view of Cibolo Creek Country Club.
Photo courtesy of Judy Cathey-Treviño

entertainment complex. Denny opened the hall with $13 in his pocket and a case of beer. For the next ten years Cibolo Creek Country Club focused its entertainment policy on hiring hardcore country to deep blues to Texas songwriters to zydeco acts. Texas high school coaches held several meet and greet sessions, and numerous benefits for various causes have taken place there. A benefit was held for Junior Mitchan, Bob Wills' last bass player, and money was raised to help defray some medical expenses. Junior donated a sweat stained seven-and-one-fourth-inch Stetson hat that Bob Wills had given him that was auctioned at the event.

Denny eventually took over sole ownership and grew weary of working his day job and running a dance hall at night. A fan appreciation month celebrating ten years in business showcased some of the top Texas music acts at the hall. Cibolo Creek Country Club went out in style when it closed its doors. Country rocker Joe Ely holds the attendance record. Other acts that have performed there are Delbert McClinton, Jimmie Dale Gilmore, Kimmie Rhodes, Hal Ketchum, Kelly Willis, Bruce Robison, Rosie Flores, Billy Joe Shaver, Walter Hyatt, Guy Clark, Townes Van Zandt, Ray Wylie Hubbard, Terri

Soulful Ray Wylie Hubbard at Cibolo Creek Country Club
(November 1990)

Known for penning the national anthem of "outlaw country," "Up Against the Wall Redneck Mother," Hubbard has established himself as one of Texas's most gifted songwriters and entertainers. *Photo courtesy of Judy Cathey-Treviño.*

Billy Joe Shaver and son, Eddy, at Cibolo Creek Country Club.

His songs are his legacy to the world. He has written such country standards as "Ride Me Down Easy," "I'm Just an Old Chunk of Coal," and "Honky Tonk Heroes." *Photo courtesy of Judy Cathey-Treviño.*

Hendrix, and numerous Cajun and zydeco groups. Public radio station KSTX recorded several shows that aired on their "Sunday Night Sessions" program. In July of 1998 Ray Wylie Hubbard recorded a live album at the hall.

The hall will be turned into a barbecue restaurant with plans to change the name back to Luxello Hall and hopefully feature some of the same people that the dance hall became known for.

From San Antonio take Loop N 1604 to Nacogdoches Road and go east about two miles to Evans Road and take a right, and Cibolo Creek Country Club is about a mile on your right at 8640 East Evans Rd.

Clear Springs Hall and Store

Clear Springs, Texas ~ Guadalupe County

What was once a dance hall that focused on artists who had a big hand in creating the progressive country movement of the 1970s, or as Steve Fromholz says the "Progressive Country Music Scare," is now a popular eatery called Clear Springs Cafe. Posters of Ray Wylie Hubbard, Augie Meyers, B.W. Stevenson, and Rusty Wier and the Tennessee Hat Band are on the walls of the restaurant. Built in 1874 as Clear Springs Store and Saloon, the curved rafters are similar to the ceilings at Anhalt and Fischer Halls.

This area was settled by German immigrants in the 1840s and 1850s. Named for a water source later inundated by Lake Dunlap, the Clear Springs community never evolved into a town but remained a

Photo courtesy of Judy Cathey-Treviño

Clear Springs Store, 1904

Jim Bowie discovered the springs in 1825 while surveying the area near the Guadalupe River southeast of present day New Braunfels.

In 1874, the Clear Springs Store and Saloon was built up the hill, away from the springs and sometimes surging Guadalupe River. Soon a community developed around the store and the town was named Clear Springs.

Travelers and locals alike stopped by the store for provisions, the news (gossip), and to knock back a few cold ones. The saloon, as was the custom of the day, served food along with drinks to its patrons; and the Clear Springs Cafe was born.

The "clear springs" are now part of Lake Dunlap, but Clear Springs Restaurant is still serving fine Texas cuisine at the original restaurant near New Braunfels and in Nacogdoches, Texas.

NO SEPARATE CHECKS
15% GRATUITY FOR PARTIES OF 10 OR MORE
EXTRA CHARGE FOR SUBSTITUTIONS AND ADDITIONS

Back of menu for Clear Springs Café.
Courtesy of R. G. DeWitt Jr.

rural settlement. A store built at this site in the 1870s by Johann Andreas Bruestedt became the commercial and social center for the surrounding area. A saloon and community hall was added to the building in later years. The Clear Springs Gin Company located behind the store was important to the local cotton industry. It is said that Jim Bowie, while surveying the Guadalupe River just southeast of what was later to become New Braunfels, discovered the springs in 1825.

The old stage may sit quietly now, but at one time the place was rockin' with the likes of Ray, Augie, Buckwheat, and Rusty.

From Interstate 35 in New Braunfels take Highway 46 South. Clear Springs Cafe is located approximately three miles east of New Braunfels, Texas, at 1692 Highway 46 South (830-629-3775).

Club 21

Uhland, Texas ~ Caldwell County

Located between San Marcos and Lockhart and just a few miles east of Kyle is a unique dance hall that I used to go by on my way to school at Texas A&M while traveling on Highway 21. Club 21 was purchased in 1967 by Martha Ilse, and her son William manages the bar and dance hall. The front bar dates back to 1893 with the dance hall added in the back in 1912. A nine-pin bowling alley was added in 1933. In the thirties the dance hall was used as a gym for the Uhland School and has always been a family gathering place to enjoy talk and gossip and to dance. Country bands perform every Friday and Saturday night. Don Walser's photo cover from his *Rolling Stone From Texas* album was taken there, and music videos by Keith Whitely (filmed just before he died), Jimmy Vaughan, and Tish Hinojosa also showcase the vintage dance hall. In 1980 the Oscar nominated film *Resurrection*, starring Ellyn Burstyn, had several scenes taken at the hall. Beer commercials for Coors Light and Bud Light's "Big-Hair Contest" have been filmed at Club 21. Located next to the Uhland General Store, it is on the Old Spanish Trail (Camino Real) that Spanish

Photo courtesy of Judy Cathey-Treviño

Club 21 bandstand.
Photo courtesy of Judy Cathey-Treviño

explorers traveled as far back as 1713.

Located off Farm Road 21 at the Hays/Caldwell County line, eleven miles northeast of San Marcos, Texas. Capacity-400. Live music every Friday and Saturday night. Bar open every day except Sunday and Monday (512-398-2901).

Club 281

Round Mountain, Texas ~ Blanco County

No longer open. Located north of Johnson City on U.S. 281 at Farm Road 1431.

Photo courtesy of Judy Cathey-Treviño

Coshatte Hall

North of Sealy, Texas ~ Austin County

First established as Coshatte Turnverein in 1883, Coshatte Hall continues to host family gatherings and community functions. The early settlers in the area were intrigued by the Coshatte Indian tribe that camped there and named the hall after them. This is another fine example of the "round" dance hall in southeast Texas.

Take highway 36 north of Sealy (8.5 miles) to Miller Road. Turn right and go about one mile to Nelius Road. At that T intersection turn to your left and go about half a mile to Waak Road, turn right, and go about one half mile. Coshatte Hall will be on your right.

Photo courtesy of Judy Cathey-Treviño

Cotton Club

Lubbock, Texas ~ Lubbock County

The Cotton Club was built by Rob Lowe in the 1940s and was first a popular attraction for big bands such as Benny Goodman, Harry James, and Guy Lombardo. The West Texas venue had a seating capacity of around 1,400. Its booking policy leaned towards country acts during the 1950s as the area enjoyed a boom in the oil field industry. Hank Thompson, Ray Price, and rock and roll star Little Richard were some of the stars who entertained at the Cotton Club during this period. Bob Wills lived a short time in nearby Amarillo during the 1950s and became a featured performer at the Cotton Club on many Friday night dances. Two of America's greatest influences on popular music, Elvis Presley and Lubbock-born Buddy Holly, entertained there early in their careers. Presley played two shows, April 29 and October 15, 1955. The Cotton Club burned down sometime in the latter part of the decade.

Coupland Dance Hall

Coupland, Texas ~ Williamson County

Coupland was founded in 1887 by Civil War major and former Travis County sheriff Theodore van Buren Coupland. Once known as La Casa Grande Ballroom, Coupland Dance Hall has served as a mercantile shop and was featured in the movies *Lonesome Dove*, *A Perfect World*, and *Cadillac Ranch*. The bar in the dance hall was built in 1886. Coupland was a thriving railroad town at that time. The building surrounding the bar was constructed in 1904, and the dance floor was added in 1936. The hall measures 7,000 square feet. Johnny Gimble,

Photo courtesy of Judy Cathey-Treviño

Johnny Bush, Johnny Rodriguez, Hank Thompson, Willie Nelson, Jerry Jeff Walker, Gene Watson, and Gary Stewart have played at the hall.

Coupland is located between Taylor and Elgin off Highway 95, twenty-five minutes out of Austin. "It's just a two-step back in time." The dance hall is at 115 Hoxie in Coupland (512-856-2226). Owner, Barbara Worthy.

Crider's Rodeo and Outdoor Dance Pavilion

Hunt, Texas ~ Kerr County

Crider's is located north of Kerrville along the Guadalupe River, in Hunt, Texas. They proclaim to have been the longest running dance venue in Texas until it closed briefly in 1994. Established in 1925 by the Crider family, it is now owned by Laverne Crider Moore. Crider's is known for its massive oak tree that towers above the outdoor

Photo courtesy of Judy Cathey-Treviño

dance area. The oak caught fire in 1993, and efforts were made to save it by lifting a portion of the tree with cranes and attaching heavy wire on several large limbs to lessen the load on the tree. Jacks have also been used to help support the tree, and it actually appears to be doing better.

A rodeo is held in conjunction with the dances, and not much has changed throughout the years. Several generations have enjoyed the tradition that the Crider family started. Wilton Crider, whose father established Crider's, was influenced by Jimmie Rodgers and makes a point to sing his idol's songs. When Wilton was nine years old he had the opportunity to meet Rodgers in Kerrville, where the two lived. "I met him fishing on the Guadalupe River. He was very kind to me, and I'll always remember the famous train conductors hat he was wearing."

Adolph Hofner recalls playing at Crider's with Wilton's dad sitting on a chair by the bandstand all evening.

The area is also home to several boys and girls camps that add to the population each summer.

To get to Crider's, from Kerrville take Highway 27 through Ingram and curve around onto State Highway 39, which goes directly through Hunt. Crider's is on the left next to the rodeo arena. Open May through September every Saturday night (830-238-4874). Owner, Laverne Crider Moore.

Crystal Chandelier

New Braunfels, Texas ~ Comal County

George Strait once played a New Year's Eve dance at the Crystal Chandelier. The dance hall closed several years ago and has now been converted into Rudy's Barbecue and an Italian restaurant.

Located on Highway 46 in New Braunfels just a few miles west of Interstate 35.

Photo courtesy of Judy Cathey-Treviño

Crystal Springs Dance Pavilion

Fort Worth, Texas ~ Tarrant County

The dance hall was owned by Sam C. "Papa" Cunningham and was named for the cool and clear springs that surfaced from the ground. With low ceilings and a capacity of close to 1,000, it drew large crowds to hear Milton Brown and others.

Crystal Springs was never the same after Brown's untimely death in 1936 although it remained a popular nightclub through the 1950s. It closed in 1959, laying dormant until it reopened in 1965. A year later it was destroyed by a fire.

The hall was located northwest of downtown Fort Worth at 5336 White Settlement Road.

Crystal Springs Dance Pavilion (1925).
Mrs. Sam (Hattie) Cunningham is standing at the doorway.
Photo courtesy of Hank and Donna Cunningham

Crystal Springs Dance Hall and Pavilion and The Musical Brownies
(September 1932)

The Crystal Springs shuttle bus was used to pick up and drop off patrons from downtown Fort Worth. It was also used for touring. Standing: Sam C. "Papa" Cunningham (owner of the hall). Inside the bus, left to right: Henry Cunningham (bus driver), Ocie Stockard, Milton Brown, Derwood Brown, Wanna Coffman, and Jesse Ashlock. *Photo courtesy of Hank and Donna Cunningham.*

Dessau Dance Hall and Saloon

Dessau, Texas ~ Travis County

Dessau Hall was built in 1876 by a German immigrant from Dessau, Germany, for area residents to enjoy as a community center. It is the oldest live music venue in the area. Austinites commonly refer to the hall in north Austin as "Broken Spoke North." Big bands such as Tommy Dorsey and Glenn Miller played there. Bob Wills, Hank Williams, Ernest Tubb, and Patsy Cline played their Texas swing and country music years ago. In 1954 a young Elvis Presley performed to just a handful of people before he went on to bigger things.

A fire destroyed the original hall.
Photo courtesy of Judy Cathey-Treviño

Harry Choates and Floyd Tillman with their "babes" Dessau Hall, late 1940s.
Photo courtesy of Floyd Tillman

The most unique feature of the dance hall was the pecan tree that once grew in the middle of the hall and out through the roof. The Persinger family purchased the facility and re-opened it after it had remained dormant through the eighties and early nineties. It was leased out for "College Night" during the late eighties. When the big bands played, house rules were enforced.

"No Spittin' On The Floor, No Hats Inside, And No Cuss'n"

The Marshall Tucker Band, Kelly Willis, Joe Ely, Billy Joe Shaver, Jimmy LaFave, Terry Allen, and Guy Clark have recently performed there. With a seating capacity of 750, it is returning to its former glory days.

Dessau is eleven miles northeast of Austin and two miles southwest of Pflugerville in northeast Travis County. The dance hall is at 13422 Dessau Rd. (512-251-4421).

Devil's Backbone Tavern

Farm Road 32 ~ Comal County

A tremendous earthquake erupted over 30 million years ago in a sea-covered central Texas. Geologists believe the magnitude of the prehistoric earthquake, with forces deep within the earth, was so powerful that it pushed, shifted, ripped, and tore up lands that

Photo courtesy of Judy Cathey-Treviño

Devil's Backbone Tavern bar area.
Photo courtesy of Judy Cathey-Treviño

separated the terrain into two regions; the Edwards Plateau (Hill Country) and the lower Gulf Coast plains. The divide resulting from this is called the Balcones Fault Line. It was named by Spanish missionaries exploring Texas. The majestic views of the area seen from the edges of the fault line made it appear as if they were looking at the site from a stretch of balconies. Part of this natural phenomenon formed a spiny crest of gnarled hills that Indians and Spaniards would visit to seek spirituality and gold. This is the Devil's Backbone.

Considered one of the most haunted places in America, there have been hundreds of ghost sightings recorded there over the years. The most famous sighting has been of a young woman holding a child and walking up and down the Devil's Backbone, crying for her lost husband. Ranchers in the area have reported seeing the face of "Drago," the American Indian warrior. Ghost story author Bert Wall witnessed an entire Civil War battle from the top of the Backbone. He was featured on a segment of television's *Unsolved Mysteries* in 1996.

The winding, razor-backed ridge makes for one of the most scenic drives in Texas. It extends from Ranch Road 12, just south of Wimberley and west some twenty-four miles close to the town of Blanco. Eighteen miles east of U.S. Highway 281 is the Devil's

Backbone Tavern. Built in 1932, the dance hall was added to the structure in the early 1950s. Owners Rick and Helen Ferguson have hosted one of the longest running songwriting sessions in the area. These sessions started on April 7, 1994, and an acoustic jam session takes place every Friday evening. Helen stated that they enjoy folks coming back to the tavern to discover that it has not changed or bowed to commercialism. Every day somebody drops by and asks about the myth of the Devil's Backbone.

The Devil's Backbone Tavern is open every day. Songwriters meet each Wednesday, and the acoustic jam takes place on Friday evenings, out on the patio. Located eighteen miles east of U.S. 281 on Farm Road 32 close to Wimberley, Texas (830-964-2544).

Die Halle Dance Hall/ Schramm Opera House

Industry, Texas ~ Austin County

Industry, in Austin County, is known for being the first permanent German settlement in Texas. Johann Friedrich Ernst was granted land by the Mexican government in 1831, and the area prospered with the growth of various crops, with tobacco being the primary one. It was the active cigar industry that is responsible for the town's name.

Die Halle was built around the turn of the twentieth century and was the focus for dancing, plays, and costume balls. It resembled a "big red barn" with the interior decorated with ornate nickel-plated lamps that hung from the ceiling. In Lavern Rippley's book *Of German Ways* she states that Germans "bequeathed to America their zest for harmless pleasure. The name 'Opera House' was used to avoid the stigma that Puritanism had attached to the word 'theater,' implying some kind of sinful enjoyment."

The hall, located on Main Street in Industry, was purchased by the Herman Schramm family around 1908 and later converted into a family residence.

Photo courtesy of the County Historic Commission's book:
Dance Halls of Austin County

The Farmer's Daughter

San Antonio, Texas ~ Bexar County

The Farmer's Daughter was founded by Bobbie Barker in October of 1961. She brought to the dance hall country music's biggest performers. She was brutally murdered on September 23, 1982. The crime has remained unsolved.

Lefty Frizzell, Ernest Tubb, Loretta Lynn, Bob Wills, George Jones, Willie Nelson, Merle Haggard, Kitty Wells, Buck Owens, Porter Wagoner with Dolly Parton, Marty Robbins, Johnny Duncan, Ray Price, Johnny Bush, Adolph Hofner (who played "The Daughter" every Wednesday for twenty-five years), Charlie Pride, Mel Tillis, Jim Reeves, Slim Whitman, and Hank Thompson were just a few of the huge names that were hired by Barker to play the Farmer's Daughter.

Photo courtesy of Judy Cathey-Treviño

Billy Gray and The Western Oakies

Popular western swing band in the 1950s, Gray was once Hank Thompson's bandleader. Left to right: Lloyd Jordan (bass), Bobby McBay (drummer), Merle David (fiddle), Norma Beasley (vocals), Billy Gray, Leon Thomas (steel guitar), Leon Bullinger (fiddle, mandolin), Bill Carson (lead guitar), and Bucky Meadows (guitar, piano). *Photo courtesy of Dewey Glen "Bucky" Meadows.*

Johnny Rodriguez played his very first show there, and it was also the first place Asleep at the Wheel played in San Antonio.

Contracts from the American Federation of Musicians were framed on the walls in addition to pictures of the artists. On June 15, 1962, Slim Whitman was paid $400 against 60 percent of the door. July 3, 1963, shows George Jones receiving $650 against 60 percent. September 19, 1963, has Hank Thompson getting $600 against 60 percent. Merle Haggard received $650 against the percentage, and in 1968 Willie Nelson was guaranteed $800 against the percentage.

The IRS closed down the Farmer's Daughter in April of 1996. It reopened as the Farmer's Daughter Steakhouse not long afterwards, closed again, and opened yet again as the New Farmer's Daughter. In the summer of 2000 the Farmer's Daughter was closed once more, and at this writing no one else has attempted to revive the old dance hall.

Bands performed Wednesday through Sunday. A 2:00 P.M. and 7:00 P.M. dance was featured each Sunday. The dancers would keep the bands on their toes, because they remained on the dance floor in a dancing position between songs.

There was a huge picture of Bob Wills located by the bar. In November of 1961 Bob Wills' Texas Playboys were the first band to play there. Wills did not attend the show. Tommy Duncan fronted the band while Wills was in a hospital recuperating from a mild heart

DON'T MISS

Farmer's Daughter

PRESENTS

CAPITAL RECORDING ARTIST

BUCK OWENS

AND THE

BUCKAROOS

One of America's Best Versatile Dance Band

Thursday, November 14

··· **LATEST HITS** ···

"*Foolin' Around*" "*Act Naturally*"
"*Under Your Spell Again*" "*Love Gonna Live Here*"

For Reservation Call ED 3-7391

Buck Owens 1963 poster at the Farmer's Daughter.
Poster courtesy of Ray Sczepanik

attack. He spoke to the audience, through the sound system, by phone from his bed, thanking everyone for coming out and wishing he could be there with them.

Bob Wills (1967) performing for the
Farmer's Daughter 6th anniversary celebration
Photo courtesy of KBUC Radio

The bar had a capacity of about 500 and was located in southeast San Antonio at 542 N. W.W. White Road.

Fischer Hall

Fischer, Texas ~ Comal County

The area of Fischer was settled by Hermann Fischer in 1853 after establishing a general store to service the community in the Devil's Backbone region of Texas. Originally called Fischer Store, the word "Store" was dropped in 1950, and the community became known as Fischer at that time. A post office was established in 1876, and descendants of the original owners still operate it.

Fischer Hall was built sometime after the post office was opened,

Fischer Hall
Photo courtesy of Judy Cathey-Treviño

and it is said to have been built by a one-eyed carpenter. The quaint hall has curved rafters in the ceiling and a beautiful stage area on the east side. Willie Nelson's movie *Honeysuckle Rose* had several scenes filmed at the dance hall and a Nashville music video by Wade Hayes was filmed there as well. Adolph Hofner stated that Fischer Hall was where he "kinda got his start" in the music business.

Next to the hall is a community hand-set nine-pin bowling alley that is still operated by a local club, a reminder of pastimes enjoyed by German pioneers. Nine-pin bowling focuses on team points instead of individual scores, and pins are set in a diamond shape pattern, instead of a triangular one. The game originated in Central Europe and was popularized by monks. Central Texas is home to approximately nine-teen nine-pin bowling alleys. The Fischer Agricultural Society established a school and bowling club in the 1880s, and the school later became Fischer Hall.

Fischer Hall is located near the intersection of Ranch Road 32 and FM 484, on Fischer Store Road, roughly 20 miles west of San Marcos. The hall can be rented out for private parties. The Annual Christmas Dance is the social event of the year.

Floore Country Store

Helotes, Texas ~ Bexar County

Floore Country Store (pronounced Floor) was established by John T. Floore, a big man who stood six feet five inches, after he decided to take a leave of absence from the Majestic Movie Theater that he managed in downtown San Antonio. Brought up in East Texas, he moved to San Antonio in 1928. His leave of absence from the Majestic Theater became a permanent one after he settled in Helotes (Spanish word for corn), northwest of San Antonio. He ran a grocery store, started the first newspaper in the area, and developed Floore Subdivision before building the dance hall and outdoor patio that bears his name. Floore Country Store opened in 1946.

Being aware that Helotes and Bandera (with the Silver Spur and

Grand opening of Floore Country Store, 1946.
Photo courtesy of Steve Laughlin

Cabaret prospering) were well known for country music, he felt that
another venue would help cater to the folks traveling back and forth
from San Antonio to Bandera.

Floore's reputation as an entrepreneur has been immortalized in
a song Willie Nelson penned titled "Shotgun Willie" released on his
album of the same name. While living in East Texas, Floore made
money off the Ku Klux Klan. Floore and a lawyer friend sold sheets
and hoods to members for eight dollars.

John T., Willie, and Paul English, Willie's longtime drummer, had
a partnership in the Willie Nelson Music Company. The business
arrangement stipulated that Willie play at Floore Country Store once
a month and not play elsewhere in the immediate area. These days
Willie still comes back to play there at least once a year. John T. and
Willie had a father-son relationship, and Floore even accompanied
Willie on a trip to Carnegie Hall. On October 3, 1975, John T. passed
away at the age of seventy-seven in a room adjacent to his famous
country store. Before he died he had sold his business to his cook, Joe
Algueseva, in 1973. Joe and his wife, Estella, and daughter Lydia con-
tinued to hire bands and offer the "World's Best Homemade
Tamales," bread, and country sausage. Joe and Estella decided to

John T. Floore and Willie Nelson, 1969.
Photo courtesy of Steve Laughlin

retire in 1990. Their desire to sell the business to someone who would keep the tradition that the Alguesevas successfully managed to keep going uninterrupted was most important. They found that person when they sold the business to Steve Laughlin.

Steve grew up in Helotes and ironically knew the booking of the music business from his experience working at the Majestic Theater. Steve and his parents C.B. and LaVerne along with Steve's son Jake run Floore Country Store with the same traditions that John T. established. One of Willie Nelson's many shows at Floore Country Store took place on April 7, 1991, and was special in many ways. It was one of the first shows he did with his band after the trouble he had with the Internal Revenue Service. It had rained for several days before the show, and Sunday was the first day the weather had eased up a bit. Overcast and with the possibility for more showers, there was doubt if the show would go on or not. The crowd was there though, and everyone was hoping to see Willie perform. Just as Willie walked

Front entrance to Floore Country Store.
Photo courtesy of Judy Cathey-Treviño

from his bus to the stage the sun suddenly broke through the clouds
for the first time all week, and three and one half hours later, Willie
finished his last song.

The outdoor patio, billed as the largest in the Southwest, accom-
modates around 2,000 people. Rainy nights or cold weather brings
bands inside where about 400 folks can be accomodated. The outdoor
stage was enlarged in 1996, and a metal roof replaced the wooden one
above the bandstand. Dances are held each Friday and Saturday with a
Sunday dance declared "family night" where everyone gets in with no
cover charge.

Willie Nelson and Johnny Bush used to play at Floore as members of Ray Price's Cherokee Cowboys. Darrell McCall and Roger
Miller were Cherokee Cowboys earlier in their careers and performed there when they became stars in their own right. Bob Wills,
Ernest Tubb, Lefty Frizzell, Hank Williams Sr. and Jr., Johnny Cash,
Tammy Wynette, and Waylon Jennings are a few of the many great
names who have performed there over the years. When Roger Miller
lived in San Antonio he dropped by many times and entertained with
whatever band was playing that night. George Chambers has played

Johnny Gimble at Floore Country Store

Johnny Gimble joined Bob Wills and His Texas Playboys in 1949. Born and raised in Tyler, he was voted "Instrumentalist of the Year" by the Country Music Association in 1978. *Photo courtesy of Judy Cathey-Treviño.*

Robert Earl Keen at Floore Country Store, 1993.
Photo courtesy of Lawrence "Doc" Beck

Gary P. Nunn at Floore Country Store

Nunn was designated official "Ambassador to the World" by Texas governor Mark White in 1985, who proposed that the song "London Homesick Blues" become the official state song of Texas. *Photo courtesy of Lawrence "Doc" Beck.*

Floore Country Store since 1959. He recalls backing up Willie and Roger on many occasions.

Entertainers who have recently performed there are Merle Haggard, Ray Price, Johnny Bush, Delbert McClinton, Robert Earl Keen, John Prine, Gary Stewart, John Anderson, Lyle Lovette, The Texas Tornados, Asleep at the Wheel, Moe Bandy, Gary P. Nunn, and Jerry Jeff Walker. On June 18, 1999, George Jones played the historic venue for the first time, breaking Merle Haggard's attendance record. Competition from the San Antonio Spurs NBA finals game, played the same night at the Alamodome, did not affect his performance as 3,300 fans watched this great legend entertain.

Former President George Bush and actors Patrick Swayze, Jimmie Smits, and Meg Ryan have dropped in as customers. Part of the movie *8 Seconds* was filmed there as well as several television shows and commercials. *Sixty Minutes* was there to film Willie in 1996.

Douglas Wayne Sahm and Jake Noll Jr.

Born November 6, 1941, in San Antonio, Doug Sahm made his radio debut at the age of five. He teamed together with Augie Meyers to form The Sir Douglas Quintet in 1965. Billed as a British invasion band, their song "She's About a Mover" became an international hit. In 1989 Sahm, Meyers, Freddy Fender, and Flaco Jimenez formed the Texas Tornados and mixed country, rock, Tex-Mex, norteno, and R&B. Sahm died on November 18, 1999. He is pictured on the left at Floore Country Store with Jake Noll Jr., guitar technician for the Tornados. *Photo courtesy of Judy Cathey-Treviño.*

A pool table and small arcade are set up by the jukebox on the east side of the hall. Jukeboxes are in most of the dance halls today with vinyl records replaced by compact discs. Pictures of many entertainers who have performed there are on all the walls of the hall. There are several pictures of John T. from hunting and fishing successes.

The humor of John T. Floore can be seen in the many signs that decorate the building. "We may not be the world's worst, but we keep trying," "Try our old tough steak and wilted vegetables," "Lookers welcome, especially good lookers." Outside a sign still markets Willie's Sunday shows that he used to play earlier in his career.

Located in Helotes, Texas, just north of San Antonio on Highway

Legendary Vox keyboardist and
accordionist Augie Meyers at Floore Country Store.
Photo courtesy of Judy Cathey-Treviño

16. John T. Floore Country Store, 14464 Old Bandera Rd., Helotes, Texas, (210-695-8827). Open Friday, Saturday, and Sunday. Lunch served from 11 a.m.-2 p.m. Monday through Friday.

Freiheit Country Store

Freiheit, Texas ~ Comal County

Freiheit is a German word for freedom, and the tiny town of Freiheit, Texas, is located just northeast of New Braunfels. It first originated in 1891 as the San Geronimo School Community.

Freiheit Country Store is home of original Texas music. Built around 1890, the store is famous for serving award-winning hamburgers and for showcasing Texas songwriters. Mo Humble hosts the

Outdoor stage area, Freiheit Country Store
Photo courtesy of Judy Cathey-Treviño

Texas Songwriters' Radio Showcase every Saturday at the store. His show *Humble Time* records various songwriters and broadcasts these tapings on several radio stations at a later date. The sessions capture a live performance that Mo always seems to get motivated. *Humble Time* takes place every Saturday from 2:00 P.M. to 6:00 P.M.

Shorty and Rosie Haas took over ownership of Freiheit Country Store in 1982 and gave it new life.

From San Antonio take Interstate 35 North to New Braunfels. As you leave New Braunfels go approximately one and a half miles to exit 191 and follow the service road to FM 483. Take 483 to the right and follow it to FM 1101 and take a right. Freiheit Country Store will be just down the road on your right (830-625-9400).

Frydek Pleasure Hall/Svinky Hall

Frydek, Texas ~ Austin County

Built by Joe Pavlecek, who later owned Mixville Sunrise Hall, it was sold to Joe Svinky in the late 1920s. Rancher, businessman, and musician Louis C. Sodolak purchased the hall in 1940 and immediately disassembled the building.

Frydek Pleasure Hall (on left) with band.

Front row, left to right: unknown, Louis C. Sodolak, Joe Buchala, unknown, Frank Vancik, and Joe Micak. Back frow, left to right: August Micak, Frank Micak, Anton Micak, unknown, Louis Micak, and John Micak. Photo courtesy of the County Historic Commission's book: *Dance Halls of Austin County.*

Garfield Dance Hall

Garfield, Texas ~ DeWitt County

This community, located sixty plus miles southeast of San Antonio, was named for president James A. Garfield. The red dance hall is similar in construction to nearby Nordheim Dance Hall. Built in 1892, a year after the Garfield Gun Club was organized, it has a cupola to aid in venting out hot air and allowing the current of cooler air to flow when all the windows are open during the summer months.

Take Highway 72 from Nordheim toward Yorktown and take a left on Farm Road 952. Go about five miles through Cotton Patch, and there the road turns into Farm Road 2656. Just four more miles and Garfield Hall is on your left.

Photo courtesy of Judy Cathey-Treviño

Grapetown Dance Hall

Grapetown, Texas ~ Gillespie County

Grapetown Dance Hall is nestled in the hills in an old German community between the towns of Comfort and Fredericksburg off the old San Antonio Road. German immigrants helped settle the community in 1848 with most of them making their living as freighters. They would take their produce by wagon from Fredericksburg through San Antonio to Indianola, now a ghost town, and on to the Gulf Coast. In 1887 the Old San Antonio and Aransas Pass Railroad was completed at the town of Comfort. The high divide at Mt. Alamo between Comfort and Fredericksburg in Kendall County forced the railroad to continue west to Kerrville and scrap plans to connect to Fredericksburg. Other interests organized the Fredericksburg and Northern Railway Company, and by 1913 the railroad finally reached Fredericksburg. A quarter-mile-long tunnel was excavated through

Photo courtesy of Judy Cathey-Treviño

the Mt. Alamo Divide, and the first railroad tunnel in Texas was created. The railroad tunnel is located off the Old San Antonio Road next to Grapetown. Each day before sunset about one million Mexican freetailed bats blacken the skies and help get rid of the insect population in the area, as they make their way out of the abandoned tunnel. The Texas Parks and Wildlife Department has designated the tunnel and home of the Mexican freetailed bats as a natural preserve. The 920-foot-long tunnel is at the entrance to the old Davenport Ranch. Hondo Crouch's ranch adjoined the back part of the property.

Grapetown has had a singing and shooting club since 1870. The dance hall is rented out for celebrations during the year, and each Labor Day the end of summer is acknowledged with a dance and music celebration called the *Dast Ist Alles Festival*. Proceeds from this event have helped needy musicians offset medical bills. At the turn of the century, the city of Cain, located six miles south of Grapetown, also had a dance hall. All that remains in Cain today are several residences and vacant store buildings.

To get to Grapetown go east on Highway 290 out of Fredericksburg and take Grape Creek Road to the right (south). Grapetown is about eight miles on your left.

Gruenau Dance Hall

Gruenau, Texas ~ DeWitt County

The green sea of grass on the prairie flowing back and forth reminded early settlers of green ocean waves as they approached this area of southeast Texas. The suffix "nau" is a German word meaning nautical.

The Gruenau Turnverein was organized on May 1, 1898. A hall was built in 1900 with dances held once a month. Maifest and harvest festivals were established by 1909. Riflemen teams competed with nearby communities followed by a dinner and the crowning of Schuetzen-Koenig (King of the Riflemen). A grand parade followed the ceremonial activities. By 1927 the Verein saw the need for a new

Photo courtesy of Judy Cathey-Treviño

hall as the area grew, and with a $10,000 loan from a Mr. Anton Koopman, members hired day labor to build the hall, with building construction supervised by Herman J. Buchhorn. Buchhorn had supervised the completion of Lindenau Hall the previous year. Building materials were brought in by wagons from Yorktown, and everyone marveled at the octagon shaped structure with intricate woodwork and the center pole that supported the roof and ceiling. The hardwood maple floor and hand cut rafters were painstakingly crafted by excellent carpenters.

The Babe Schindler Orchestra played the grand opening dance at the hall. Governor of Texas James Ferguson visited Gruenau Hall in 1932, and on April 25, 1948, the Texas Top Hands played the fiftieth anniversary celebration of the Verein.

The hall was expanded in 1965 with more floor space added to the north side of the building. A bolt of lighting struck the top center pole, shattering one third of the supporting structure in 1986. Fortunately no fire damage resulted from the hit of lighting, and the sagging roof was eventually repaired with the help of two retired "roughnecks," who had experience working on drilling rigs from high elevations. With their knowledge and with the help of others, the roof was lifted back into place as the center pole was repaired.

From Yorktown take Highway 72 to Highway 119 and go left three miles to Farm Road 108. About three more miles, Gruenau Road and the hall are on your right. Gruenau Hall is visible shortly after you turn on 108.

Gruene Hall

Gruene, Texas ~ Comal County

Gruene (pronounced green) was renamed for the prominent early settler Heinrich D. Gruene, son of Ernest and Antoinette Gruene, a German couple who settled in New Braunfels in 1845 to farm. Heinrich built a mercantile store, cotton gin, and a bar and social hall for the local farmers to enjoy. The town, first known as "Goodwin," prospered in 1872 with 8,000 acres of cotton. Gruene's cotton gin was

Photo courtesy of Judy Cathey-Treviño

Interior view of Gruene Hall
Photo courtesy of Judy Cathey-Treviño

powered by water from the Guadalupe River and was replaced after being destroyed by fire with the state's first electric-powered gin. It has been turned into the Gristmill Restaurant.

Gruene at one time was on the main stage road from San Antonio to Austin. What is now The Gruene Mansion Inn was formerly Heinrich's home. It was purchased by Bill and Sharon McCaskill and refurbished in detail to its former days. The old mule stall has been converted into a bed and breakfast facility overlooking the Guadalupe River, along with several other buildings. The Gruene Mansion is on the National Register of Historic Places.

Gruene died in 1920, and not long afterwards the boll weevil killed the cotton crop. Business in general took its toll from the Depression as well. In 1976 Pat Molak and Mary Jane Nalley bought the dance hall and gristmill and brought it back to life. The dance hall was reopened in 1979. Beer has been served there since 1878. Affectionately known as the "oldest dance hall in Texas," it has been a getaway for college students from Southwest Texas, UT, and Texas A&M as well as for tourists from around the world.

Many country performers have cut their teeth while playing the Hall. Before George Strait became the huge superstar he is today, he had played Gruene Hall for six years. His first album cover photo was taken inside the hall. Lyle Lovette honed his writing skills there, as did Hal Ketchum and Robert Earl Keen. Hal was a carpenter during the day and performer at night, and he lived in Gruene for eight years before he left for Nashville. Jerry Jeff Walker, Joe Ely, Delbert McClinton, Steve Earle, Rodney Crowell, Garth Brooks, John Hiatt, Ernest Tubb, Ray Price, Leon Russell, Arlo Guthrie, Merle Haggard, John Prine, Junior Brown, Kris Kristofferson, Gary P. Nunn, Ray Wylie Hubbard, The Texas Tornadoes, and Townes Van Zandt are just a few of the many stars who have played the hall. On December 3, 1998, Willie Nelson performed a benefit for flood victims in New Braunfels. This was his first official show at Gruene Hall.

Black and white glossies of many of these artists adorn the walls. It is interesting to see the record labels these artists were on before signing with larger record companies. Clint Black, Travis Tritt, and David Ball have all used the venue as a backdrop for their musical

Chris Wall at Gruene Hall
Photo courtesy of Lawrence "Doc" Beck

Americana Music Jam (May 3, 1998)
Poster courtesy of KNBT Radio

videos. The movie *Michael*, starring John Travolta, had several scenes filmed there.

The wooden dance floor has been worn to a polish from all the two-steppin' over the years. Burlap sacks hang from the ceiling to absorb some of the acoustics. The hall holds about 500 people.

Take Interstate 35 north, turn left at exit 191 (west on Farm Road 3060), turn left at the first stoplight, and follow the road to Gruene. The hall is right in town on Hunter Road.

Harmonia Hall (a.k.a. Zapp Hall)

Warrenton, Texas ~ Fayette County

Warrenton, Texas, located twelve miles northeast of La Grange, was founded by William Neese, who named the town after Warren Ligon, a prominent storeowner. A post office was established in 1837, and the community grew to a population of 100. Warrenton has the

Photo courtesy of Judy Cathey-Treviño

distinction of having the world's smallest Catholic church, St. Martin's. The church measures 12 x 16 feet and has become popular with tourists who also visit several antique shops in town. From La Grange take State Highway 237 for 12 miles into Warrenton. Harmonia Hall is on Highway 237.

Harmonie Hall

Shelby, Texas ~ Austin County

Named for 1822 settler David Shelby, the town of Shelby grew up around the mill of German pioneer Otto Von Roeder. The Ohlendorfs, Vogelsangs, Rothermels, and Vanderwerths arrived in 1845. The post office opened in 1846 with Shelby as postmaster. A school was built in 1854, and an agricultural society, singing society, and a band were started shortly afterwards. The decline of farming forced residents to

Photo courtesy of Judy Cathey-Treviño

Shelby Harmonie Hall in 1883
Photo courtesy of the County Historic Commission's book:
Dance Halls in Austin County

move and search for other means of support.

Harmonie Hall was built by Oswald Palm. There is an annual New Year's Dance, and the second weekend in April and October draw many visitors to Shelby for a big antique show at the hall.

From Nelsonville take Highway 159 through Industry to Farm Road 1457, go right five miles to Shelby, and go left on Farm Road 389. Harmonie Hall is on your right.

Henry's Hideout

Fetzer, Texas ~ Grimes County

Henry Phillips built the bar in 1937 and added the dance hall in 1964. The establishment has been passed on to Henry's nephew, Billy. Henry's is famous for having over 6,400 antlers on the ceiling, proclaiming itself as "the horniest place" in Texas. Local bands play each Friday and Saturday night with special events such as the brisket

Photo courtesy of Judy Cathey-Treviño

cookoff celebrated each May. Veteran Texas performer Rusty Wier entertained for the cookoff party on May 6, 2000.

Henry's Hideout is located 20 miles north of Cypress between Magnolia and Plantersville on Farm Road 1774 in Fetzer, Texas, in southeast Grimes County (281-356-3538). Open 11:00 A.M. - 2:00 A.M. 7 days a week. Billy Phillips, owner.

Hermann Sons Hall

Poth, Texas ~ Wilson County

Ray Sczepanik recalls seeing George Jones at the hall in 1964. It is now owned by the Non Emmanuel Assembly of God.

Poth is seven miles southeast of Floresville at the junction of U.S. Highway 181 and Farm Road 527. Go to Town Square off Highway

181 to Sutherland Ave. The hall will be at the intersection of Sutherland and Dickson.

Photo courtesy of Judy Cathey-Treviño

Hye Dance Hall

Hye, Texas ~ Gillespie Country

The community of Hye, located ten miles west of Johnson City, is
named for Hiram G. (Hye) Brown, who first established a post office
and general store in 1886. He built a larger facility across the road in
1904 to serve the needs of the growing area. The Deike family has
owned the general store since 1923. Postmaster Levi Deike and his
wife, Ruby, have run the general store and post office for many years.
Levi grew up in a stone house located a few yards from Hye Dance
Hall. There is a picture of the Deike family, in baseball uniforms,
hanging in the store. Nine brothers and a sister as a substitute player
were enough family members to field their own team.

Lyndon Baines Johnson, whose boyhood home is close by, used the front porch of the store to appoint Lawrence F. O'Brian as U.S. Postmaster General in 1965. LBJ mailed his first letter from there at the age of four. Ruby inherited post office box #276 that once belonged to President Johnson.

Ruby recalls her father telling her that he came to dances at the hall in horse drawn wagons as a teenager around 1915.

The hall has been used for storage in recent years but now houses Aqua Aire Industries. You can faintly see the painted advertisement on the front of the hall that reads "Dance Next Saturday Night."

Hye is located on Highway 290 about ten miles west of Johnson City, five miles east of Stonewall, Texas, and just east of Ranch Road 1 that goes in front of the LBJ Ranch.

Photo courtesy of Judy Cathey-Treviño

Kendalia Halle

Kendalia, Texas ~ Kendall County

Kendalia Halle was built in 1903 by the Nicholas Syring Musical Club, as a place to perform and entertain the small community. The band consisted of Oscar Kneupper, Adolph Kneupper, Henry Kunz, Willy Ludolph, Phillip Lux, and Nicholas Syring. Later the Zoeller Band played there for seventeen years. At one time there was a bowling alley, a barbershop, and a cotton gin by Kendalia Halle. It was an active community in the Hill Country, and the hall was used for wedding receptions, graduation ceremonies, reunions, and school plays.

Kendalia Halle is a thirty-minute drive from Loop 1604 that circles around San Antonio and off Highway 281 North. Coming from San Antonio on 281 you take FM 473 west and go seven miles to the junction of 473 and 3351.

Photo courtesy of Judy Cathey-Treviño

Back of Kendalia Halle
Photo courtesy of Judy Cathey-Treviño

Years ago the small portion to the right of the stage was fenced off with chicken wire. This is where the nonpaying customers would sit and watch and not be allowed to dance. The paying customers would use this part of the hall to bed down their children while they continued to dance. Dances would begin during the day and last until the next morning, with everyone bringing food to share with one another. Traveling was done by horse and buggy, so going to these dances took quite a bit of effort.

When the windows are propped open during the summer months and the fans are on, a nice current flows through the hall. The dance floor is actually two in one. A second hardwood floor was built on top of the pine floor in the 1930s. A decision was made to add a new oak floor on top, rather than removing the old floor. Local resident Emil Kneupper helped lay down the oak floor as a young man. The hall measures 60 x 40 feet. Benches still surround the walls as they did when the hall first opened. A beer garden was added on to the east side of the building several years later. James Zoeller visited Kendalia in 1997 and recalled going to dances with his parents when he was six

Interior of Kendalia Halle
Photo courtesy of Judy Cathey-Treviño

years old. He would sleep under the benches while his parents danced all night.

Tom and Glenda McKinney managed Kendalia Halle from 1996 to 1999. Vera D'Spain, in a letter to Tom and Glenda, wrote that her father, Paul Kneupper, Uncle Herman, and third cousins Charley and Edgar Kneupper were in some of the bands that first played at Kendalia Halle. Adolph Kneupper wrote his name and date on a rafter over the bandstand. It is not known if it was written before or after he fell off the roof when helping build the hall.

The oak tree out front was used to chain unruly customers if they were fighting or causing problems. They were usually released after they had sobered up. One night a fight broke out and one of the band members, not wanting to get hurt, jumped out a window behind the stage. Although not injured in the fight, he hurt himself in the fall.

A draw curtain was used across the stage when community functions were held and is now on display at the Kendalia library.

The red fir wood used to build the dance hall was shipped from Oregon by railroad to Boerne, Texas. It was then brought to the site by horse drawn wagons. The wood provided great acoustics for my

Nicholas Syring Musical Club in front of Kendalia Halle, early 1900s
Photo courtesy of Tom McKinney

Live From Kendalia Halle recording that we released on September 27, 1997.

Lee and Dallas Temple purchased Kendalia Halle in 1996 and kept it as a family place to visit. Their slogan was "I'd rather be dancing at Kendalia Halle." Kendalia Halle closed in 1998.

> Sometimes when we are resting after cleaning the hall, we try to imagine people over ninety years ago coming to the hall and dancing or just listening to the music. What a beautiful sight that must have been. The people in those days didn't have all the things that we have to entertain ourselves with, and music and dancing was their favorite pastime. We cannot relive the past, but we can enjoy the pleasures that were so dear to our ancestors
>
> Tom and Glenda McKinney

Kendalia Halle is located at the junction of Highways 473 and 3351, eight miles south of Blanco and 7 miles west of 281 North. Owners, Lee and Dallas Temple.

KJT Hall (Lodge #6)

Dubina, Texas ~ Fayette County

Just east of Schulenburg in southern Fayette County lies the oak filled community of Dubina, known as the first Czech settlement in Texas. During the time of the Civil War, resident Augustine Haido was drafted into service, although he did not believe in the Confederacy's cause. Haido later became the first Czech lawyer in the United States. He was also responsible for renaming the town, first known as Navidad, to Dubina. Dubina is a Czech word for oak grove.

After the railroad bypassed the community, not long after the Civil War, the area's population started to decline.

The KJT Hall Lodge #6, located next to a beautifully restored Catholic church and surrounded by massive clusters of oak trees, is characterized by a facade on two sides of the hall. The initials KJT are

Photo courtesy of Judy Cathey-Treviño

from Czech words *Katolika Jednota Texaska,* which mean Catholic Union of Texas. It became the first organization to insure Czech men of Texas (mutual insurance company). The roof's dome type structure gives the old building a unique character. The outhouses on the grounds take you back to a different time when luxuries of today did not exist.

Dubina is located five miles east of Schulenburg in south Fayette County on Farm Road 1383.

KJT Hall

Ammannsville, Texas ~ Fayette County

Noted farmer and architect Andrew Ammann was the first settler to arrive in this area southeast of La Grange in southeastern Fayette County. With the help of German and Czech immigrants, the

Photo courtesy of Judy Cathey-Treviño

community was established in the 1870s and Ammannsville prospered with several stores, saloons, and a couple of blacksmith shops
and cotton gins.

The KJT Hall became a focal point for the people of
Ammannsville.

During the late 1940s, Texas Czech bands became extremely popular in South Texas. Beginning with Frank Baca (pronounced Bacha)
in the late nineteenth century, Texas-Czech music began to show
European influences in the state. Frank Baca is said to have had the
first Czech band in Texas. An immigrant from Czechoslovakia, his traditions were followed by his son Ray and then his grandson Gil. The
Gil Baca Band performed at Richard Nixon's inaugural. Other
Texas-Czech bands that played the hall were the Joe Patek Orchestra
and the most popular of all, Adolph Hofner.

KJT Hall is located in Ammannsville, which is nine miles southeast of La Grange on Farm Road 1383.

Knipper's Store and Dance Hall

New Braunfels, Texas ~ Comal County

Knipper's Store and Dance Hall is actually in the small town of Comal
just west of New Braunfels. The old building still stands even though
it is no longer open.

From San Antonio take 1604 to FM 2252 (Nacogdoches Road) and
go northeast past FM 3009 to where FM 2252 goes right but Old
Nacogdoches Road continues straight. Stay straight on Old
Nacogdoches Road for three more miles and the road runs into FM
482. Knipper's is there at the T intersection.

Photo courtesy of Judy Cathey-Treviño

Kosciusko Dance Hall

Kosciusko, Texas ~ Wilson County

The settlement of Kosciusko (pronounced Kachoozko), with its community center and beautiful St. Ann's Catholic Church, was named after General Thaddeus Kosciuzko (proper spelling of his last name) who was a hero of the American Revolution. From Poland, Kosciuzko was educated in his homeland and studied engineering in Paris. He arrived in America in 1776 and before long was commissioned as a Colonel of Engineers by the Continental Congress after helping fortify battle sites that eventually became turning points for America against the British. He became good friends with Thomas Jefferson and distinguished himself even more by building and fortifying West Point, New York. In 1783 General George Washington appointed him

Photo courtesy of Judy Cathey-Treviño

Brigadier General. Kosciuzko returned to his native Poland and helped his country win freedom from surrounding European countries. After returning to America in 1797, he received a hero's welcome. His residence in Philadelphia is a national memorial to this hero of the American Revolution.

The dance hall/community center was converted from a gymnasium in 1938. The gym also served as an auditorium for the school that was located between the hall and St. Ann's Church. The school was torn down after it was incorporated with nearby Poth High School. In 1974 the hall was remodeled and enlarged. Monthly dances are held at the dance hall, and a dance kicks off the Stockdale Rodeo each year.

From San Antonio take Interstate 10 east to Seguin, go right on 123 south through Stockdale to Highway 541. Go right on 541 and the hall is one mile on the right.

KT Dance Hall

San Antonio, Texas ~ Bexar County

Mrs. Leroy Field learned how to dance as a young girl at KT Hall. Dancing became part of her life as she grew older, attending many dances at Macdona, Quihi, Anhalt, and KT Hall. The waltzes and two-steps she learned in the late 1930s were from German bands performing at KT Hall. As she reached her teenage years, her parents never worried about her going out to dances. They knew that she was busy having fun on the dance floor and not driving around at night. KT Hall later became a clock shop and is now used to store antiques. Located in San Antonio at 2017 Austin Highway.

Photo courtesy of Judy Cathey-Treviño

La Bahia Turnverein

La Bahia, Texas ~ Washington County

This area is named for the county road that passes by the hall. La Bahia is Spanish for "the bay." Settled in the 1870s by German immigrants, they soon organized a turnverein, which is still active today.

La Bahia is in southwest Washington County just a quarter mile from State Highway 237 and is fourteen miles southeast of Brenham.

Photo courtesy of Judy Cathey-Treviño

Liedertafel Fireman's Hall

Sealy, Texas ~ Austin County

Ferdinand Lux and F. Kinkler Jr. sold the land where Liedertafel Hall is to the "Liedertafel" Singing Society. Society members helped build the octagon-shaped hall in 1914. It was sold in 1945 to the Sealy Volunteer Fire Department, and the hall has recently been restored.

Take Texas Independence Trail from Sealy (North 36) to the west end of Main Street at Lux and Peschel Road.

Photo courtesy of Judy Cathey-Treviño

Lindenau Rifle Club (Lindenau Schutzen Verein)

Lindenau, Texas ~ DeWitt County

In 1891 German farmers settled in this area, which Charles and Daniel Wild named "Lindenau." A saloon owned by William Buckhorn was one of the first establishments in Lindenau. A shooting club was organized in 1901, and members built a long hall next to the saloon. The main purpose of the Lindenau Schutzen Verein (rifle club) was for rifle practice, but members also gathered for dancing, singing, theatricals, and card and domino playing. Marvin Olle inherited a Winchester .32-caliber WCF rifle that belonged to his grandfather, August William Olle, who was a member of the verein. It was used during turkey shoots where the birds were placed in cages and marksmen had to shoot off the heads of the turkeys as they stuck

Photo courtesy of Judy Cathey-Treviño

Rifle Club members in front of the old Lindenau Dance Hall, date unknown.
Photo courtesy of Marvin Olle, whose grandfather is somewhere in the picture

their heads out of the cages. The top marksman in the shooting competitions known as "Koenig Feast" was crowned king and a celebration followed with a sausage supper. A May Queen was elected by votes for ten cents during May Feast celebrations. The King and Queen festivities were discontinued after World War I.

Lindenau was once located approximately one and one half miles northwest from its current location. After the Galveston, Harrisburg and San Antonio Railroad companies established rail service from Cuero to San Antonio in 1906, members of the rifle club moved the hall to where it is today. The old hall was rebuilt in 1926 on land donated by Fritz Kuester, and at that time members changed the name from "Lindenau Gun Club" to Lindenau Rifle Club." The hall had large doors that opened on the south and north side of the building with a smaller structure located next to it for mothers to take care of their babies.

An eating stand was located by the hall, and wives of the members helped make and serve potato salad, cabbage slaw, vegetable dishes, and desserts. A popular attraction at the hall was the "maypole dance," where a pole was placed in the ground and crepe paper streamers were attached to the pole for little girls to dance around as they held onto the streamers. When the new highway was built close to the hall, these shooting exhibitions ceased. The hall is still used for wedding receptions, Sons of Hermann meetings, and for private gatherings

Lindenau is located on Farm Road 953 and is five miles northwest of Cuero.

London Hall

London, Texas ~ Kimble County

Planned as the court square of a proposed county, the town was platted about 1878 by Postmaster Len L. Lewis, whose town name choice "Betty Lewis" (for his wife) was vetoed by the postal authorities. The name "London" is thought to have been proposed by the Pearl family,

Photo courtesy of Judy Cathey-Treviño

LEGENDARY
LONDON HALL
HOME OF COUNTRY-WESTERN DANCING
LONDON, TEXAS

London Hall bumper sticker
Courtesy of London Hall

for their old Kentucky hometown.

On the western cattle trail, London had trail drivers as residents and sold supplies to crews passing with longhorn herds. In the early days there was a blacksmith shop, stores, cotton gin, three churches, and a school. Coke R. Stevenson, Texas governor from 1941 to 1947, lived in London as a child.

Billy Ivey owns the hall that was established by her father, Ty Bo Ivey. A small room was added next to the dance hall for pool players and beer drinkers "who don't care to dance, but enjoy listening to the bands play." On each table in the hall, tin pie pans are used as ash-trays. Black and white photos of Johnny Duncan, Darrell McCall, Frenchie Burke, Johnny Bush, Clay Blaker, Johnny Gimble, and Hank Thompson are located at the front entrance. In the front bar, where more pool tables and a cozy stone fireplace are located, are posters of Adolph Hofner, The Texas Top Hands, and Jimmie Martin and The Texas Plow Boys. Words to the "Ballad of London Hall," written by Johnny Bush and an official memorandum from the state of Texas pro-claiming "Jimmie Rodgers Day," can also be found in this side room by the dance floor.

George Chambers has played in most of these dance halls since the late 1950s. He was also a teacher who once taught biology to Steve Earle, at Holmes High School in San Antonio. He recalls play-ing a "deer hunters dance" at London Hall several years ago, and one of his band members asked George if he wouldn't mind going to the bar and getting him a drink. George was busy setting up equipment for the night and asked why he couldn't get it himself. Well, the band member stated that some hunters by the bar were making fun of his hairstyle and he was afraid of them. After the show, band members loaded up most of those hunters who were heckling the band members and took the drunk men on the bus back to Junction to a motel where the hunters and the band members were staying.

Located 18 miles northeast of Junction, Texas, on Highway 377. Owner, Billy Ivy (915-475-2296).

The Longhorn Ballroom

Dallas, Texas ~ Dallas County

This was a traditional honky-tonk with no fancy tablecloths or mirrored balls. The Longhorn was built in 1950 by O.L. Nelms as the Bob Wills Ranch House. Tax problems with the venue forced Bob Wills to give up the venture. It was managed in 1952 by Jack Ruby (Lee Harvey Oswald's assassin). Dewey Groom reopened it after it had been closed for a while and brought entertainers such as Roy Acuff, Webb Pierce, Jim Reeves, Willie Nelson, Carl Smith, Johnny Gimble, Mel Tillis, Lefty Frizzell, Asleep at the Wheel, and Kitty Wells to the ballroom. The Longhorn Ballroom has been closed for a number of years.

Located just southwest of downtown Dallas off Industrial Blvd. at 216 Corinth.

Longhorn Cavern Dance Hall

Burnet, Texas ~ Burnet County

Certainly the most unusual dance hall that ever existed in Texas was located below ground level, in a cave. Created by groundwater dissolving limestone and friction from rushing waters that had seeped underground around a million years ago, Longhorn Cavern is rich in geological history as well as interesting folklore. The geologic structure of these caverns (rooms) with stalactite and stalagmite formations from mineral formation was first used as a refuge by predatory animals. Comanche Indians later used one chamber to chip rock layers of chert to make tools. After Confederate soldiers drove the Indians away, it was used to manufacture gunpowder. Outlaw Sam Bass used the cavern as a hideout from law officers. Ranchers turned the "Indian Council Room," named for the chamber where the Comanches made their arrowheads and stone tools, into a dance hall. It became a popular place to enjoy the consumption of alcoholic beverages during Prohibition. With its 35-foot ceiling and constant 65 degree Fahrenheit temperature, it was a comfortable getaway. The state of Texas purchased the cavern and surrounding land in 1931 and turned it into a state park.

Longhorn Caverns is located on Park Road 4 just off U.S. Highway 281, eight miles southwest of Burnet, Texas, in southwestern Burnet County.

Lubianski Dance Hall

St. Hedwig, Texas ~ Bexar County

In the 1960s Lubianski Hall was the place to take an important date. You could go there and improve your Texas two-step with the country shuffles the band would be playing. The town site was settled by John Demmer, a native Silesian, in 1852. A post office opened in 1860 and was called Cottage Hill before the name was changed in 1877 to honor the duchess and patron saint of Silesia.

Willie Nelson, Johnny Bush, Augie Meyers, and Moe Bandy were some future stars-to-be when they played there in the 1960s. Some old-time locals still remember the first hall Albert Lubianski Sr. built in the 1920s. A shortage of parking forced him to build a "new" hall in 1949, just down the street from the original one. Dances are scheduled the first Saturday of each month with the exception of February, which honors the trail ride headed for the San Antonio Livestock Show and Rodeo. Wedding receptions and private parties are still booked at the hall. Ray Price and his Cherokee Cowboys celebrated the fiftieth anniversary of Lubianski Dance Hall in November of 1999. The Texas Top Hands, led by Ray Sczepanik, opened the festivities. Albert Lubianski Jr. ran the hall for many years. He was accidentally electrocuted while working on an air conditioning unit at the hall on June 21, 2000.

St. Hedwig is sixteen miles east of downtown San Antonio in eastern Bexar County, two miles east of Loop 1604 on FM 1346.

Photo courtesy of Judy Cathey-Treviño

Luckenbach Dance Hall

Luckenbach, Texas ~ Gillespie County

A young couple in love, a government job, and family conflict... they're all at the root of a place called Luckenbach. The story began in 1849 when August Engel and his wife started an Indian trading post on the site. The general store was built at that time, and a post office opened the next year. (Engel appointed himself postmaster after getting President Zachary Taylor to allow for an official post office in the area.) When the family petitioned for the office, one of the Engel girls, Minna, was chosen to name the postal community. She was engaged at the time to a local rancher named Albert Luckenbach. In an act of love, she defiantly went against her family's wishes and named the post office Luckenbach. Albert didn't stay in Luckenbach though. He and Minna married but later moved to a nearby community, which was seeking a post office of their own. This time, Minna became postmistress and named the postal community Albert. It must have been true love. But Albert didn't stay in Albert either, and Luckenbach went on to a fame that Minna could hardly have dreamed of.

In 1970 the Engel family decided to sell the tiny little town. They placed an ad in the Fredericksburg paper and caught the attention of Guich Koock. Guich together with Kathy Morgan and a man who became the personification of Luckenbach—John Russell "Hondo" Crouch—purchased the town. Guich sold his third ownership in 1974 to pursue a career in Hollywood as an actor-stunt man. (He portrayed a deputy in the sitcom Carter Country.) After five generations, Beno Engel had sold the town, which included a general store, post office,

Photo courtesy of Judy Cathey-Treviño

blacksmith shop, cotton gin, a small stone house, and two outhouses. The dance hall was built in 1887.

Hondo then proceeded to do what Hondo did best: have fun and encourage others to join him. Luckenbach fun came to include everything from the understated to the overstated. There were the daily versions of sittin' and whittlin', playin' dominoes, spinnin' yarns, and pickin' and singin'. Events like the Ladies State Championship Chili Cookoff, the Luckenbach Non-Buy-Centennial, and the Luckenbach World's Fair (with Willie Nelson) brought thousands of people at a time to Luckenbach. Why, it got so crowded, they had to get their own parking meter.

The motto, "Everybody's Somebody in Luckenbach" was born, and Hondo became well known as a storyteller, philosopher, and humorist. Luckenbach became the gathering place for musicians and songwriters. You were never sure who you might run into picking and singing around the wood stove or under the trees. Lyndon B. Johnson would often sneak away from his ranch ten miles away in Stonewall and visit with Hondo over a cold beer or two.

Hondo died in 1976, but the Luckenbach legend lives on. The property is still owned by Kathy Morgan and Hondo's daughters, Chris and Becky. Plans are being made for a volleyball court and a children's playground to reinforce a family atmosphere.

Luckenbach's fame was fueled by an album that was recorded live in 1973 by Jerry Jeff Walker. *Viva Terlingua* epitomized the progressive country movement that was beginning to explode in Texas. Jerry Jeff at that time was known as a songwriter foremost, having penned "Mr. Bojangles," and this transplanted New Yorker was instrumental in helping to establish Luckenbach as a town where pickers can come and relax and play their style of music for the locals. What made out-of-state tourists travel to this Hill Country haven was a song recorded by Waylon Jennings and Willie Nelson, "Back to the Basics of Love," otherwise known as "Luckenbach, Texas." The song was written by Bobby Emmons and Chip Moman after Guy and Susan Clark's description of the small community. Moman was producing Waylon at the time and presented the song to him. It became the hit single on Waylon's *Ol' Waylon* album that went platinum in 1977. Suddenly folks would drop in on that little hamlet and ask when Waylon and Willie or Willie and Waylon would be arriving. A friend of mine told me about the time he was sitting under the oak trees drinking

Lloyd Maines performing in Luckenbach
for KFAN Radio's birthday celebration.

Maines is best known as a pedal steel player but is one of the best record producers
in Texas. *Photo courtesy of Judy Cathey-Treviño.*

Willie Nelson's 1996 4th of July Picnic poster
Courtesy of Luckenbach Dance Hall

beer and listening to some locals pick and grin when someone dressed like Willie walked near the people gathered around, laid his guitar down on a bench, and walked away. Before long the buzz was "Willie is here."

Luckenbach continues to have dances and picking sessions, but in 1995 Willie decided to hold his July 4th picnic there. Over 12,000 people witnessed thirty bands perform and ignite the little town once again, and a new generation of Texas music lovers was born. Waylon performed at the 1996 picnic. This was his first visit to Luckenbach. Jerry Jeff Walker hosted a Labor Day Texas Music show that also brought in Texas music lovers from around the state. Annual events that take place in Luckenbach are: The Ladies' State Chili Bust (first Saturday in October), Hug-In (Valentines Day weekend), Texas Independence Day Celebration (March), Mud Dauber Festival (mid March), and the Bluebonnet Ball.

The highway department finally gave up the struggle to keep the "Luckenbach" signpost in place as countless souvenir hunters absconded with yet another one. And it's sad to see the old metal signs that once adorned the west wall of the store and post office vanish through the years.

The town of Luckenbach celebrated its sesquicentennial on May 30, 1999, with Jerry Jeff Walker and the Gonzo Compadres.

Luckenbach is open year round with the exception of Christmas and is always closed on Wednesdays to acknowledge livestock auctions in Fredericksburg.

Directions to Luckenbach:

From Johnson City:

Go west on Highway 290, pass through Hye and Stonewall. Look for the Grape Creek Winery on your left at South Grape Creek. Cross over the creek and continue west on 290. Look for the first paved road to your left (Luckenbach Road). Turn there and follow until you come to a stop sign. Turn left and immediately right.

From Fredericksburg:

Go east on 290. Turn right on FM 1376 (toward Boerne) at the KOA campground. Drive until you pass Behrends Feed Operation on your left. Continue east on 1376 and go right on the second paved road.

From Boerne:
From IH-10 go north on 1376 through Sisterdale. Pass PR 1888 on your right. Go around curve to your left, up the hill, and down a hill until you cross a creek. Turn left there at the first paved road.

From Blanco:
Go west on FM 1623 to FM 1888, then take a left on 1888. Follow 1888 until you come to FM 1376. Turn right, go up the hill and around the curve to left and down the hill until you cross a creek. Turn left on first pavement.

From San Antonio:
Go north on Highway 281 to Blanco and follow directions from Blanco above.

Macdona Hall

Macdona, Texas ~ Bexar County

The community was named for the owner of the town site, George Macdona. Built in 1908, Macdona Hall served as a dance hall, shooting hall, Hermann Sons Hall, and an auction barn. The last dance at the hall was in 1959. It became the Macdona Auction Barn for several years before burning down in 1986. The hall measured 120 feet long and 50 feet wide and was located just west of San Antonio, not far from Lackland Air Force Base. Records show that the dance hall was managed by Richard Magnus and Walter Koehler in 1919, and later Frank Zienert took over management duties and handed the job over to Leroy Forester in 1950.

Adolph Hofner and The Pearl Wranglers and The Texas Top Hands alternated many weekends between Macdona and the Hermann Sons Hall Grand Lodge in San Antonio. On Tuesday, December 16, 1952, The Texas Top Hands backed up Hank Williams. This was to be one of his last performances. He died sixteen days later en route to a show in Canton, Ohio, on January 1, 1953. Ray

Photo by Ida Mae Welch, courtesy of Ellen Jonas Loessberg

Sczepanik, who now leads The Texas Top Hands, has the band log-book that shows they were paid $100. Rusty Locke, the band manager/steel guitarist for The Texas Top Hands at the time, remembers that a gentleman walked Hank to the stage and said, "These people came to see you perform."

Easy Adams and Cal Berry played twin fiddles that evening, and Cal stayed busy trying to steady Hank by grabbing the back of his belt. Rusty called over the hall manager, Crash Stewart, and said that something needed to be done about "ole Hank." He looked tired and you could tell that it was not just alcohol that put him in the condition he was in. Hank played no more than thirty minutes. Williams' dependence on pain pills, morphine, and alcohol were getting the best of him. The back pain he was suffering from, due to a disease known as spina bifida occulta (where vertebral arches of the spine fail to unite), was getting more intense.

Williams did manage to perform much longer three days later at the Skyline Club in Austin. Some say it was his greatest performance. Ralph Mitchell Sr., who owned the Bandera Cabaret for forty years, had a contract already signed for a January 11th engagement, but that show never went on.

The hottest bands to play Macdona and other dance halls during

Hank Thompson and his Brazos Valley Boys at Macdona Hall in 1954
Photo by Ida Mae Welch, courtesy of Ellen Jonas Loessberg

Macdona Hall, D. Hicks, Lefty Frizzell, and Larry Nolen
Photo courtesy of Larry Nolen and Greg Holland

Bob Wills, on fiddle, performing with his Texas Playboys at
Macdona Dance Hall in 1951. Admission was $1.25.

"For Bob Wills, it was always about the music, about making it swing and making it
sizzle. He understood groove, showmanship, and the gray areas between genres
that made for the most potent musical hybrids. There was something about the way
he did what he did that's been inspiring musicians and music lovers ever since."
Ray Benson. *Photo by Leroy Fields, courtesy of Ellen Jonas Loessberg.*

that time were Bob Wills, Hank Thompson, The Texas Top Hands,
Adolph Hofner and The Pearl Wranglers, Smiley Whitley, and Lefty
Frizzell. Lefty's big hit during that time was "Always Late." He
arrived late one evening to play Macdona Hall in his new yellow
Cadillac convertible. During the show someone took lipstick and
wrote "Always Late" across the hood of his new car.

The Texas Top Hands played twenty-five to thirty nights a month
and performed five days a week on WOAI Radio in San Antonio. They
played Macdona Hall, Dessau Hall, and Floore Country Store on a
regular schedule. Rusty convinced John T. Floore to add his outdoor
patio next to the dance hall. According to Rusty, rock and roll and
drive-in movies hurt the band business at that time. As Rusty quoted
from a Bob Wills song, "Time Changes Everything." When I asked
Rusty how he managed to keep such a busy schedule, he replied, "I

Texas Top Hands (1946)

One of the state's oldest active bands. Organized in 1945 out of the breakup of the Texas Tumbleweeds, they have been led by Walter Kleypas (1945-1952), William "Rusty" Locke (1952-1955), O.B. "Easy" Adams (1955-1979), and Ray Sczepanik who is the current bandleader. Standing, left to right: Leonard Brown, William "Rusty" Locke, Walter Kleypas, and George "Knee-Hi" Holley. Kneeling: O.B. "Easy" Adams and John "Curly" Williams. *Photo courtesy of Ray Sczepanik.*

don't know how we really did it. People would ask me if I worked good hours and I told them, all of them and sometimes those hours were good ones." Other bands that played at Macdona Hall over the years were Gold's College Ramblers and Theo Arizt Orchestra (1929), American Eagles Orchestra (1947), Texas Road Runners (1950), Charlie Walker, Johnny Lee Wills, and Tex Ritter.

Macdona, Texas, is located just off 1604, eighteen miles southwest of downtown San Antonio in southwest Bexar County.

Martinez Social Club

Martinez, Texas ~ Bexar County

Managers Charles and Rosalee Mikolajczyk were married at the club in 1959. The club was founded in 1912. It has a great natural oak dance floor with a seating capacity of about 500. The hall was expanded in 1976 and a nine-pin bowling alley was moved to a separate building behind the hall at that time. Chartered members own the club. They have live bands on Wednesday, Saturday, and Sunday evenings.

From the outskirts of San Antonio take Interstate 10 east to the Converse exit (1516) and go right three miles to 1346 and take a right. The hall is located next to the Honky-Tonk Bar Association (210-344-4747).

Photo courtesy of Judy Cathey-Treviño

Mayflower Dance Hall

Rio Medina, Texas ~ Medina County

Frank A. Burrell established a saloon that had an extended pavilion overlooking the Medina River that was used for dancing. Not long after these dances became popular, Burrell built the Mayflower in 1910 next to his saloon. The twelve-sided hall measured 40 feet across with the bandstand located directly across from the front entrance. The stage area was bumped out from the hall to provide more room for dancing.

Milton Haby bought the saloon and dance hall in the 1950s. The hall was taken down board by board in the late 1950s or early 1960s. The photo of the hall was taken in 1957.

Leonard Moore runs the Texas Spirit's Saloon in Rio Medina and has renamed it The Mayflower.

The original Mayflower was located on Farm Road 471, six miles north of Castroville in Rio Medina.

Photo courtesy of Leonard D. Moore

Mesquite Hall

Lone Oak, Texas ~ Bexar County

Mesquite Hall is owned and operated by members of the Mesquite Traildrivers Association, who built the hall in 1965. Dances are held the first Saturday of the month with special dances for Halloween, Christmas, New Year's Eve, and for the San Antonio Livestock Exposition.

The Texas Top Hands, Circle C Band, and the Metheny Brothers were some of the first local bands to perform at the hall. Trail boss Chester McDougald recalls Moe Bandy, from nearby Atkins, playing with a tip bucket in front of him. Bandy has gone on to have a great career in country music, scoring ten number one hit songs and having great success with his theater in Branson, Missouri. His father was one of the founding fathers of Mesquite Hall. Frenchie Burke, Darrell McCall, Hank Thompson, and Ray Price are some of the big stars that have performed at Mesquite Hall.

Photo courtesy of Judy Cathey-Treviño

View from stage at Mesquite Hall
Photo courtesy of Judy Cathey-Treviño

From Loop 410 on the southeast side of San Antonio take Highway 87 east 7.5 miles to Loop 107 on the left and go .4 of a mile to Mt. Olive. Turn left and go .8 of a mile to Ford Road. The hall is at the corner of Ford and Mt. Olive.

Mesquite
Traildrivers
logo
*Courtesy of
Mesquite
Traildrivers*

Millheim Harmonic Verein Hall

Millheim, Texas ~ Austin County

Millheim, Texas, was established by German immigrants around 1845. Located in Austin County eight miles south of Bellville, it was first known as Muelheim and later Americanized to its present name.

The Millheim Harmonic Verein was organized not long after the Civil War Reconstruction period to continue German tradition, and the hall was built for community functions. It was built on land purchased for $15 per acre and was located next to a bowling alley and a brewery. Records in *Dance Halls of Austin County* indicate that the hall was 30 feet by 52 feet and 14 feet high. Lumber cost $20 per 1,000 feet. Barbecues, Maifest, Christmas, New Year, school plays, and Leap Year Dances were celebrated at Harmonic Hall.

The peaceful times before World War II saw the community's need for constructing a larger gathering place. Much of the lumber from the old Harmonic Hall was used to build the new hall, and its

Photo courtesy of Judy Cathey-Treviño

The Troubadours, 1929

Top row: Herman Pacher, Walter Herring, Gussie Herring, and Margaret Dittert. Bottom row: Roland Brosig, Laurence Herring, Alvin Garling, and L.L. Bender. Photo courtesy of the County Historic Commission's book: *Dance Halls of Austin County.*

grand opening was quite a celebration. It was an all-day affair with a barbecue and a big dance during the evening.

Today the hall still hosts various events highlighted by the annual Father's Day Barbecue.

Take Highway 36 north from Sealy (off Interstate 10) and go almost seven miles to Farm Road 949 and take a left. Go four miles and the hall is on the right.

Mixville Sunrise Hall

Mixville, Texas ~ Austin County

This dance hall was built in 1928 by Joe Sodolak, Vince Vancik, Frank Lastovica, and Adolph Kovasovic. Radio personality and musician Dickie McBride performed for the grand opening in 1929.

Today the dance hall is privately owned and is being used as a barn to store hay.

From Interstate 10 in Sealy take Highway 36 south about 4.4 miles to Mixville Road and go left .3 mile and the hall is on your right.

Grand opening Mixville Sunrise Hall (1929)
Photo courtesy of the County Historic Commission's book:
Dance Halls of Austin County

Dickie McBride and the Village Boys (1944/1946?)

Left to right: Dickie McBride, J.D. Stanley (lap steel), J.R. Chatwell (fiddle), Dick Jones (fiddle), Rome Landrum (drums), and Buck Henson (bass). *Photo courtesy of Mrs. J.R. Chatwell.*

Nelsonville Hall

Nelsonville, Texas ~ Austin County

Nelsonville was named for early merchant D.D. Nelson. The first Czech immigrants in Texas started arriving in this area in the 1860s. The SPJST organization (Slavic Benevolent Order of the State of Texas Society), one of the oldest Czech-American organizations in the United States, formed in this area in 1906 according to Rick Garza, who bought the dance hall in 1992. He has been trying to refurbish the building to its glory years and wants to host nonprofit organizations to help raise money for their particular needs and causes.

Photo courtesy of Judy Cathey-Treviño

The seven-foot tall windows of the hall look small from a distance, but up close you can see that they are much larger, and the warped panes of glass show its age. Advertisements above the bandstand also take you back in time when local merchants marketed their businesses at the hall. This was a common practice at most of the dance halls, and many of these signs still grace the walls, usually above the bandstand. Rick mentioned that years ago there was no competition from surrounding dance halls. They took turns having their get-togethers from one area to the other.

The original hall was built in 1905 and sometime later (date unknown) burned down. The present hall was built in 1924 on the same site.

Nelsonville is at the junction of State Highway 159 and Farm Road 2502, nine miles west of Bellville in west central Austin County.

Nordheim Shooting Club Dance Hall

Nordheim, Texas ~ DeWitt County

First known as Weldon Switch, the community's name was changed to Nordheim in 1897. It was named for a town in Germany.

One of the area's first bands, the Nordheim Brass Band, was organized in 1902 and played their music at nearby Pilot Knob Hill. Pilot Knob Hill once served as a lookout post for Indians and early settlers. Its 400-foot elevation is the highest on line between Houston, San Antonio, and Waco. Social activities moved to Nordheim after it was established, and the Nordheim Brass Band played their German style music there until they broke up in 1972.

The Nordheim Shooting Club is a product of the area's German heritage and community Mayfest celebrations of the nineteenth

Photo courtesy of Judy Cathey-Treviño

century. The Nordheim Fortschritt Verein (Progress Club) was organized in 1897. Another organization, the Nordheim Scheutzen Verein (Shooting Club), was formed in 1902. The two clubs merged in 1927 as the Nordheim Shooting Club. The present hall replaces earlier structures on the same site.

Nordheim is seven miles west of Yorktown near the Karnes County line on Highway 72. To get to the hall take Broadway off 72 for one half mile.

Old San Felipe Town Hall

San Felipe De Austin, Texas ~ Austin County

San Felipe was the first Anglo-American capital of Texas. It came into being on July 26, 1828, as capital of the Austin Colony by decree of the Mexican government. Stephen F. Austin, the Father of Texas, had begun under the 1821 grant from Mexico the settlement of more than

Photo courtesy of Judy Cathey-Treviño

1,000 families in this first American town in Texas. William Barret Travis and Sam Houston also lived here.

The Old San Felipe Town Hall was built in 1842, as the first Austin County Courthouse. It is recognized to be the oldest government building in Texas. It functioned as a school from 1880 to 1952 and has been used for many activities and dances throughout the years.

San Felipe is on the banks of the Brazos River at the Old San Antonio Road crossing on Interstate 10 just two miles east of Sealy.

Palacios Pavilion

Palacios ~ Matagorda County

Palacios is nestled along Tres Palacios Bay on the southern coast of Texas, located about 110 miles southwest of Houston. Palacios is a Spanish word for palace and is known as the "Shrimp Capital of Texas." Three different pavilions have occupied sites in Palacios on Commerce and Fourth Street beginning in 1904, and each has served as a historic symbol for the Gulf Coast and Matagorda County.

The original pavilion was designed by Victoria architect Jules Leffland and was built on a pier extending 400 feet into the bay. Called the "Pleasure Pavilion," it was a two-story open-air pavilion structure with the central portion of the lower deck used for dancing and basketball games. An outer section of the complex floor consisted of a 20-foot space that was used for skating and as a walkway. The pavilion was complete with bathhouses, which were a necessity as bathing suits in those days were not worn in public except for swimming in the bay waters. It was the social center for the "City by the Sea." Slides and diving boards were used by swimmers who enjoyed the hard and smooth bay bottom that was without oyster shells and broken glass bottles. Boat sailing was another popular activity on the bay. The Pleasure Pavilion sustained hurricane damage in 1915, 1919, and 1934 and was razed in 1935 and replaced with a new structure called the "Roundhouse."

The new pavilion was built 100 feet closer to the shoreline, was dome-shaped, one story, and its roof was supported by steel girders. The Roundhouse Pavilion continued to be the focal point of community activities, especially during the war years of the 1940s when famous big bands performed for our soldiers.

In 1961, on a date that will forever be remembered by coastal inhabitants and the world, Hurricane Carla passed through Palacios on September 11 with 200 mph winds and 17-foot tidal waves. The Roundhouse Pavilion was completely destroyed. The storm traveled hundreds of miles north with heavy rains and wind. A smaller open-air pavilion was built in the 1970s and continues to serve the "City by the Sea."

Panna Maria Dance Hall

Panna Maria, Texas ~ Karnes County

Panna Maria is the oldest Polish settlement in America. Its name is derived from the Polish words meaning Virgin Mary. The Immaculate Conception Catholic Church is topped by a cross that was brought

Photo courtesy of Judy Cathey-Treviño

from Poland by the original colonists. The community invited Pope John Paul II to visit the settlement on his trip to the United States in 1987, but time did not permit the Pope to travel there.

Adolph Hofner played the hall many times, and people still remember the great times they had at his dances.

Panna Maria is near the junction of Farm Roads 81 and 2724, four miles north of Karnes City, fifty-five miles southeast of San Antonio.

Pat's Hall

Fredericksburg, Texas ~ Gillespie County

The counterpart to Braun Hall in the 1950s and 1960s was Pat's Hall, where baseball games were played on ball fields next to the dance halls. The Texas Hill Country Baseball League played games on Sunday afternoons and were broadcast by KNAF Radio Station, sister station to Texas Rebel Radio KFAN, when the Fredericksburg Giants hosted their games. When the great Hall of Fame pitcher Dizzy Dean was stationed at Fort Sam Houston in San Antonio, he played on the ball field next to Pat's Hall while touring with the U.S. Army baseball team. Lyndon Johnson played there while in high school representing Johnson City.

First known as Seipp's Dance Hall when it was built in the 1920s, it was changed to Pat's Hall when sold to Pat and Pauline Patranella in 1953. It became popular for the hall itself and the outdoor patio dance pavilion. George Chambers commented on his experience when he played Pat's. "If you wanted to play the dances you took one 30-minute break. Bands would begin the night playing 9:00 P.M. to 11:00 P.M. and finish the evening with the last set from 11:30 P.M. to 1:00 A.M. Special yearly dances drew larger audiences, and you were required to play four hours without a break. If you did not adhere to these rules, then you never played Pat's Hall again. Thanksgiving, Christmas, and New Year's Eve dances drew at least 800 people. During winter months, bands played inside, and from May through September, dances were held both in the hall and on the outdoor patio."

Pavilion bandstand
Photo courtesy of Judy Cathey-Treviño

Slim Coleman, who grew up in Fredericksburg, said that Pat had a table reserved for him inside and also outside, at a table that had an oak tree growing through it. "My favorites were Jimmy Heap and Johnny Bush, and I have fond memories of seeing my hero 'Gentleman' Jim Reeves at the Cabaret in Bandera." Slim ran track with Arkey Juenke while in high school in Fredericksburg. Arkey is now better known as Arkey Blue. Slim said Arkey could run like a rabbit.

The sound quality inside Pat's was not very good. The concrete bricks that the hall was rebuilt with after a 1947 fire that killed three people were not very conducive for good acoustics. Pat's Hall always closed during Lent and reopened to record-breaking crowds. Hondo Crouch would often come out to Pat's to dance, drink, and have a good time, and occasionally George Chambers would end up taking Hondo home on the band bus. Hondo continued to party and would sing Spanish songs before being dropped off at the front gate of his ranch.

Pat's Hall closed in 1985. Ray Price, Johnny Bush, Willie Nelson, Adolph Hofner, Hank Thompson, Jack Greene, Tommy Duncan, Darrell McCall, Asleep at the Wheel, Moe Bandy, and George Strait all played at Pat's. The baseball diamond backstop barely stands today. The bleachers are long gone, and the old Pat's Hall now serves as a warehouse for the Shearer book publishing company.

Fredericksburg is located west of Austin on Highway 290. Pat's Hall is located on a small country lane west of town. Take West Main Street to Bowie Street and go left just about .6 miles to Post Oak. Go left on Post Oak and you'll see the old patio, with the giant oak in the middle, on your right.

Peter's Hall (Austin County Gun Club Hall)

Peters, Texas ~ Austin County

Originally called Peter's Hacienda Schuetzen Verein, its name was changed to Austin County Gun Club in 1943. This is yet another fine example of the carpentry skills of Joachim Hintz. He built and designed the hall in 1900 with help from members of the association. As with the other octagon-shaped halls he built, he suspended the roof with a center pole that allowed more room for dancing. Mayfest, skeet shooting, and monthly dances were held regularly at the hall.

Photo courtesy of Judy Cathey-Treviño

Today many social functions continue with Mother's Day celebrated annually where they serve a barbecue dinner and have a dance. Community chili cookoffs and domino tournaments are also enjoyed at Peter's Hall.

Located five miles north of Sealy, Texas. Take the Texas Independence Trail (36 North) from Sealy to Trenckman Road. Turn left and the hall will be on your right about one mile.

Pipe Creek Dance Hall

Pipe Creek, Texas ~ Kendall County

Once Lipan Apache country, Pipe Creek is said to have been named after a settler dropped his pipe in a creek when Indians were pursuing him and he managed to pick up his pipe and flee successfully. Pipe Creek was founded in 1878 by William J. Hamilton. Adolph Schott

Photo courtesy of Judy Cathey-Treviño

built the dance hall in 1930, and it served the community as a dance hall, skating rink, movie theater, and as a place for Mormons to gather each Sunday when they had no place to meet. The hall is now used as a storage facility for Pipe Creek Junction Café, located next door. Pipe Creek is 12 miles west of Boerne and eight miles south of Bandera on Highway 16.

Po-Po Family Restaurant (Nelson Dance Hall)

Welfare, Texas ~ Kendall County

Rancher and dairyman Edwin Nelson built Nelson Dance Hall in 1929, and it quickly became a popular attraction, hosting dances once every two weeks. During Prohibition, no alcoholic beverages were allowed inside the hall, but outside you could purchase "moonshine" for twenty-five cents a glass. If the glass of bootlegged nectar wasn't

Photo courtesy of Judy Cathey-Treviño

enough, you could get a gallon for three dollars. Dances usually lasted from 8:00 P.M. to 2:00 A.M. with a twenty-five-cent cover charge. The Depression eventually took its toll on these gatherings as it became more difficult for folks to spend money for gasoline and admission to the dances.

Edwin "Ned" Houston bought Nelson Dance Hall in 1932 and started a restaurant that he named Po-Po Cafe. He named it after the Mexican volcano, Popocatepetl. Ownership of Po-Po transferred to Willie Reinhard in 1934 and several others in the following years before Luther and Marie Burgon bought the restaurant in 1950. It soon became a very popular establishment, drawing people from San Antonio and all parts of the Texas Hill Country to enjoy fine country family dining. The Burgon's passion for collecting plates, as reminders from their yearly travels is evident on the walls of the restaurant. On display are over 1,450 plates, with many donated by customers and friends.

Nelson Dance Hall brought people from Boerne and Comfort to enjoy music and dancing. A rivalry between the two towns instigated many fights. One patron enjoyed fighting every Friday night. Buzz Morgenstern recalls seeing a man at dances around San Antonio who never drank, smoked, cussed, and probably never danced, but he loved to fight. David Zettner remembers playing in some halls that did not have a backstage door to escape if a fight broke out, so to make things more relaxed, he painted a door on canvas and nailed it to the backstage wall. When he played bass for Willie Nelson and a fight erupted, Willie would shout to the band "play louder." Paul English, Willie's drummer, would twirl his pistol on his drums until the fight was over. "You could see a fight break out in a corner of the hall and spread like a cancer through the crowd in no time at all."

At The Mule Barn Inn, a popular dance hall that was once located by the San Antonio Stockyards, a fight broke out during a performance by honky-tonk legend Ted Daffan during the 1930s. Daffan's wife, Lela, was whisked away and placed behind the stand-up bass, and when things settled down she was escorted back to her seat. This probably became more of a fire drill in some instances, but she was never harmed. Ted's daughter Dorothy remembers attending dances years later with a girlfriend who would hop on the back of the "enemy" and hang on to give a better advantage to her friends involved in the ruckus.

Jerry and Jenny Tilley have owned Po-Po Restaurant since 1983 and continue to offer fine family country dining in the former dance hall. Their specialty is still Marie Burgon's "Southern Fried Chicken."

Open Tuesday through Sunday. 11 A.M. to 10 P.M. Closed Mondays.

Located six miles north of Boerne. Take Interstate 10 north from Boerne and exit the Welfare exit number 533 and go about one-half mile on FM 289 (830-537-4194).

Possum Creek Inn

Theon, Texas ~ Williamson County

Immigrants from Austria, Bohemia, Germany, Moravia, and Silesia settled the community of Theon in the 1880s to 1890s. A post office named "Theon" (Greek for "to God!") opened in 1890.

Photo courtesy of Judy Cathey-Treviño

Possum Creek Inn was built in 1896, and dances in conjunction with rifle contests were established at that time. The rifle range is still located behind the hall. Possum Creek Inn is now owned by Debbie Cole and her husband. "We are truly very lucky considering the Inn's history," stated Debbie.

Saturday dances continue at the Inn. It can hold about 250 people and is open Thursday through Sunday.

Located 34 miles north of Austin, take Interstate 35 north to Highway 972 and go right for three miles to Farm Road 1105, then left two miles to Theon. Possum Creek Inn will be on your left.

Quihi Gun Club

Quihi, Texas ~ Medina County
(Pronounced Queehee)

At first the little girl seemed to be mimicking the young couple dancing next to her, but after I saw her circle the 90' by 150' dance floor, I realized that she was practicing the two-step. She had her dance steps

Photo courtesy of Judy Cathey-Treviño

down perfectly as she glided around the floor over and over throughout the evening. The tradition remains alive. Families bringing their children to a place where they learned to dance years before.

The Quihi Gun Club dance hall is located in northeast Medina County. It is balanced on a six-foot-high pier and beam foundation to keep the Quihi and Hondo Creeks from flooding the hall (during the forties the dance hall floor was soaked from the two rising creeks and in 1997 flooding waters reached just below the floor). Surrounded by ancient oak trees, the hall was built in 1890 as the Quihi Schuetzen Verein and it is one of the oldest continuously running gun clubs in the United States. Members have met each month since 1890.

Shooting clubs can be traced back to thirteenth-century Bavaria. The original forefathers brought competition shooting with them to Texas. Accurate marksmanship was a necessity for protection and to provide food for families. These events were some of the biggest celebrations of the year. Winning marksmen were paraded around the communities, and a dinner and dance were held in their honor. Minutes to meetings were written in German up until WWI. Members, which are 680 strong, receive death benefits. Whenever a member dies, their family receives one dollar from each member to help defray burial expenses.

Up until the late sixties no hats were allowed to be worn in the hall. Patrons used to place their hats on wooden pegs on the walls. Doyle Weber, former manager of the hall, remembers that when he was growing up, no boots were allowed on the dance floor either because most boots in those days had nails that would scratch up the wooden floor. The oak boards look as if they were installed yesterday and it rates as one of the best dance floors in Texas.

Acoustic material was applied to the ceiling to give the hall a great sound. Seating capacity is around 500, and they have dances two Saturdays per month. There are water coolers located inside and water hoses cooling the tin roof outside during the hot summer months. Steel guitar player Don Pack, from San Antonio, remembers on his first visit to Quihi Dance Hall chicken wire was still in place in front of the bandstand, which was once located on the west side of the hall. "You could see imprints of beer and whiskey bottles imbedded in the wire, and fortunately no one that evening tried to test it."

Henri Castro, a Frenchman of Jewish faith and Portuguese ancestry, contracted with Sam Houston and the Republic of Texas to bring settlers from Europe in exchange for a large grant of land west of San Antonio. He was very successful in recruiting his people from the Rhine Valley. The only other person to bring in more settlers was Stephen F. Austin. The first group of settlers began arriving in September 1844, and Castroville was established. One month later Castro surveyed the town site of Quihi, and ten families from Castroville moved to Quihi five months later with Indians killing two entire families. Indian raids continued until 1874.

In 1847 a Mrs. Schorobiny was kidnapped and her brother was killed. She was shot by two arrows and left for dead when she tried to escape from the Indians. She managed to crawl to town and survived the raid and lived the rest of her life in Quihi.

Quihi gets its name from the Indian word "Keechee," which is what they called the Mexican eagle buzzards that were numerous in the area. The Spaniards, who were the first Europeans to come through the area, spelled the name Quichi with the same pronunciation. The German settlers that arrived with Henri Castro dropped the C, and the pronunciation became what it is today.

Quihi is located nine miles northeast of Hondo in northeast Medina County at the intersection of Farm Road 2676 and Quihi Creek.

Redland Hall

San Antonio, Texas ~ Bexar County

Jim and Hazel Davidson built Redland Hall in the early 1980s as a place to enjoy one of their favorite activities—square dancing. Due to health reasons encountered by Jim, the hall was sold to Jerry and Cheryl Grote in 1997. The Grotes' love for dancing was re-established, and they have strived to honor the Davidsons by continuing to host square dances.

The hall is approximately 10,000 square feet with a 6,000-square-foot "floatin'" dance floor.

Jerry graduated from high school in San Antonio and immediately

Photo courtesy of Judy Cathey-Treviño

pursued a career in baseball. He was the catcher on the 1969 "Miracle New York Mets" baseball team that included Hall of Fame pitchers Tom Seaver and Nolan Ryan. Grote remembers learning to dance at nearby Luxello Hall when he was ten years old.

Redland Hall hosts the Pioneer Opry every second Thursday of the month with great country entertainment and "good clean family fun."

Redland Hall is located at 18747 Redland Road, just off Highway 1604 on the north side of San Antonio (210-499-0808).

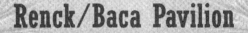

Renck/Baca Pavilion

Warrenton, Texas ~ Fayette County

This old Czech hall was moved from Fayetteville to Warrenton around 1989. Baca (pronounced Bacha) was moved by a Mr. Renck and is now popular for the antique shows held at the hall.

Renck/Baca Pavilion is located on State Highway 237, twelve miles north of La Grange.

Photo courtesy of Judy Cathey-Treviño

Reo Palm Isle

Longview, Texas ~ Gregg County

The Reo Palm Isle first originated as Mattie's Ballroom in the 1930s. It has remained a popular Longview landmark, hosting the biggest names in country and big band music.

Longview, settled in the early 1880s, got its name after surveyors working on the Texas and Pacific Railroad were taken back by the long distant view from the town site.

In 1976 *Texas Monthly* magazine named the Reo Palm Isle "Dance Hall of the Year," and the Associated Press named it "Best Club" in Texas in 1975. *CBS News* featured the hall on three different segments. The East Texas tradition hosted the top big bands of the era

Photo courtesy of Laura E. Treviño

with the Glenn Miller and the Tommy Dorsey Orchestras performing there. Two of the twentieth century's biggest stars, Frank Sinatra and Elvis Presley, graced its stage.

Elvis made four appearances at Reo Palm Isle in 1955. Research of documents, letters, and memorabilia conducted by biographer Peter Guralnick and archivist Ernst Jorgensen, by permission of the Elvis Presley estate, chronicles day-by-day tour dates from Presley's private, rare, and forgotten moments of 1955. The book *Elvis in Texas, The Undiscovered King 1954-1958* by Lori Torrance and Stanley Oberst is a wonderful look into Elvis's early years in the Lone Star State. Their research uncovered his first appearance at the Reo Palm Isle Club and what went on that Thursday evening on January 27. Disc jockey Tom Perryman, who had befriended Elvis in November of 1954, convinced owner Glen Keeling to book the future "King of Rock and Roll." Keeling had never heard of Presley. With a seating capacity of 1,800, a small crowd of around 160 attended the show, and a disheartened Elvis pondered his future in the music business.

Working on the Louisiana Hayride in Shreveport (a little more than fifty miles from Longview) and performing on package shows to help market the Hayride allowed Elvis to tour extensively throughout the state. Before the year ended he was just beginning to explode

Elvis Presley at Reo Palm Isle, Longview (1955)

A road weary Elvis performs at the Reo Palm Isle dance hall. The date on the photo, 1954, is incorrect. The sunburned arm of steel guitarist Jimmy Day from an all-day drive with his arm hanging out the window probably coincides with his August 11 date as chronicled in Elvis's day by day activities for 1955. *Photo courtesy of lifetime friend of Jimmy Day, David Zettner, who questioned Day about his suntan in picture.*

Legendary steel guitarist Jimmy Day

Some of the country stars that Day recorded and performed with were: Lefty Frizzell, Ray Price (Day's steel can be heard on "Crazy Arms"), Willie Nelson, Elvis, and Hank Williams. Jimmy Day passed away on January 22, 1999. *Photo courtesy of Dewey Glen "Bucky" Meadows.*

across the nation with his career and not long afterwards became a household name.

Performing around ninety show dates in football stadiums, baseball parks, auditoriums, rodeo arenas, and dance halls across Texas, the "diary like" memoirs give detailed accounts of these shows and exhibit a calm before the storm prior to his sudden rise to fame. Elvis played Dessau Hall, The Skyline Club, Cherry Springs Dance Hall, and five shows at the Sportatorium in Dallas that year. Ed McLemore's Big "D" Jamboree, broadcasting live on KRLD radio and originating from the Sportatorium wrestling arena, helped propel Elvis's career in Texas.

The Reo Palm Isle is located on State Highway 31 and Farm Road 1845 in Longview. Open six days a week, dance lessons on Thursday night. Capacity 2,500 (903-753-4440).

Richland Hall

Cele, Texas ~ Travis County

Cele is located north of Manor, Texas, in northeastern Travis County. The tiny community is said to have been named after the daughter of a local storeowner, Lucille Custer. Richland Hall has served this area for years and has been well cared for by the people in this quaint little community. Richland Hall still has dances scheduled throughout the year.

Richland Hall is two miles west of Farm Road 973 on Cameron Road, seven miles north of Manor.

Photo courtesy of Judy Cathey-Treviño

Rihn's Place

LaCoste, Texas ~ Medina County

Originally known as Fernando, the post office changed the name in 1898 to LaCoste after a prominent businessman from San Antonio by the name of Jean B. LaCoste.

Built around 1910, Rihn's (pronounced Reen) was once a general store called Grocery Schmidt. Third generation owner Jerry Rihn has dances there about every two months.

LaCoste is five miles southeast of Castroville on Farm Road 471 in eastern Medina County. Rihn's Place is right across from the railroad tracks.

Photo courtesy of Judy Cathey-Treviño

Roaring 20s

San Antonio, Texas ~ Bexar County

Once known as the Shadowland Night Club, the Roaring 20s ballroom was purchased by Larry Herman in 1961. It was home to his orchestra for many years. The 12,000-square-foot building is located in north San Antonio on Old Blanco Road. Built in 1926, it was once a speakeasy that entertained gangsters. Legend has it that Al Capone visited the Shadowland Night Club. A secret gambling parlor was located downstairs where it was frequently raided.

The original Glenn Miller Band performed at the Roaring 20s in

Photo courtesy of Judy Cathey-Treviño

1989. Harry James, Woody Herman, Al Hirt, and Pete Fountain have played the ballroom. The 2,000-square-foot original maple dance floor was danced on by many regular customers every Saturday night. My mom and dad celebrated their twenty-fifth wedding anniversary at the Roaring 20s.

Located north of Loop 410 just off Blanco Road just before you get to Bitters Road. The hall is at 13445 Old Blanco Road (210-492-1353). Craig Herman, general manager.

Round Hall

Bell County, Texas

This dance hall was torn down in the 1950s.

Photo courtesy of The UT Institute of Texan Cultures at San Antonio,
courtesy of Hattie Cmerek

Round Top General Store

Round Top, Texas ~ Fayette County

Built in 1848, the General Store has served the community as a hardware store, grocery store, barbershop, funeral home, hotel, and dance hall. The old ballroom is upstairs, and you can still see a portion of a bandstand on the first floor. Little has changed in maintaining the original appearance. It is now an antique and gift shop that takes pride in the manufacturing of mouth-watering fudge. Owner Peggy Wood said the biggest change in the old store has been the addition of air conditioning.

Located on Washington Street in Round Top. Round Top is about eighteen miles north of La Grange on Highway 237.

Photo courtesy of Judy Cathey-Treviño

Round Top Schutzen Verein

Round Top, Texas ~ Fayette County

Seven classic dance halls are within a twelve-mile radius of the picturesque town of Round Top. Presently known for its antique and crafts events initiated by Ms. Emma Lee Turney, it has also gained popularity with classical music performances established by the International Festival Institute. The area was first known as "Townsend Settlement." The name "Round Top" is thought to have come from a local house and stagecoach stop that was characterized by a round top on its roof. It was used as a lookout point in case the arriving stagecoach needed help from Indian raiders.

Famous resident Joel Robison moved with his family to a nearby farm in 1833, and he became an Indian fighter and served at the Siege of Bexar in 1835. It is said that he was William B. Travis' last messenger from the Alamo. He fought at the Battle of San Jacinto and helped capture the Mexican general Santa Anna. The two rode together on Robison's horse as they entered camp, and Santa Anna returned the kind treatment by presenting Robison with his gold-braided vest. The vest was later used by young grooms on their wedding day before eventually being stolen. Robison later settled in Warrenton until his death in 1889.

The Shooting Club is a perfect example of the traditions of the German immigrants in establishing a local club or verein to meet the social needs of the community. The huge oak trees and gazebo on the grounds sort of frame the dance hall itself. The hall is rented out for weddings and has a few dances throughout the year.

From Houston take Highway 290 past Brenham towards Austin and turn left on Highway 237 between Burton and Carmine. You can also travel Interstate 10 from Houston or San Antonio, taking Highway 71 north out of Columbus to La Grange before taking a right off Highway 159. Round Top is 18 miles farther.

Photo courtesy of Judy Cathey-Treviño

Saengerhalle Dance Hall

New Braunfels, Texas ~ Comal County

Saengerhalle (Singer Hall) was constructed in 1959, from several army barracks that were once used at Fort Sam Houston, on land donated by Gilbert Becker for a group of German singing clubs. Five singing clubs formed a nonprofit cooperative that ran the hall until 1996. Saengerhalles were established by German immigrants to carry on the singing traditions from their homeland. Bob and Shirley Saulle bought the dance hall in 1996 and remodeled the interior and added air conditioning, modern bathrooms, ten television sets, a beer garden, and their own sound equipment. Bob has plans to build a recording facility to tape and film live shows.

Photo courtesy of Judy Cathey-Treviño

"This hall is dedicated to Texas music," stated Bob. He has hired some of the best singer/songwriters to perform at the hall with Ray Wylie Hubbard, Chris Wall, Clay Blaker, Jimmy LaFave, Lloyd Maines, Terri Hendrix, Johnny Rodriguez, Bruce Robison, Geronimo

Treviño, Gary P. Nunn, Willis Alan Ramsey, Sisters Morales, Don Walser, Ponty Bone, The Groobees, and The DeRailers having performed there since the Saulles purchased the hall.

Saengerhalle is located one mile east of Interstate 35 off Highway 46 in New Braunfels at 255 Saengerhalle Road. It is open Monday through Friday from 4:00 P.M. to midnight and on Saturday 4:00 P.M. to 1:00 A.M. and Sunday 1:00 P.M. to 10:00 P.M. 830-625-HALL (4255). Owners, Bob and Shirley Saulle.

Schroeder Hall

Schroeder, Texas ~ Goliad County

The community of Schroeder was first settled by German immigrants beginning in the 1840s. The town residents named it Germantown, to honor their heritage, but anti-German sentiments during World War I forced the renaming of the community in honor of Paul Schroeder, who was the first person from the township to be killed during the war.

Photo courtesy of Judy Cathey-Treviño

The southeast Texas town of Goliad is the birthplace of the Texas Revolution. In 1835 Texians took control over the Spanish fort Presidio La Bahia, when they overpowered Mexican troops. On March 27, 1836, General Santa Anna and his soldiers invaded the fort that was commanded by Col. James Fannin. Three hundred and forty-one men were captured and ordered executed by Santa Anna. The Goliad massacre was forever imbedded in the memories of all Texans.

Fifteen miles northeast of Goliad is a place that is rich in Texas music history. Built in 1935, Schroeder (pronounced Shrayder) Hall totals 14,000 square feet, with a 6,000-square-foot dance floor. The hall's oak dance floor came from a lumber mill in Fort Smith, Arkansas. Byron and Helen Hoff bought the hall around 1953 from F.F. Post.

There was a rumor that this was the site of Roy Clark's first dance show ever. I had the opportunity to ask Roy if this was true when I met with him at the Moe Bandy Golf Classic in San Antonio (November 1998). He laughed when I asked him if that was his first job. "No, but it was the first time I ran into chicken wire." He said that when they were setting up to perform at the hall, he asked what the chicken wire in front of the bandstand was for. Don't worry, he was told, "you'll find out about 10 P.M." Clark started his first set in front of about fifteen people, and around 10 P.M. the place was starting to get crowded. Suddenly, Lone Star longneck beer bottles began to be thrown from the crowd, and the chicken wire helped prevent serious injury to the band.

Mrs. Hoff ran the hall after her husband passed away and continued to have dances each weekend. The names of the entertainers who performed there are quite impressive. Bob Wills, Ray Price, Willie Nelson, Mel Tillis, Faron Young, Bill Anderson, Wanda Jackson, Stonewall Jackson, Johnny Bush, David Houston, Jim Ed Brown, Darrell McCall, Moe Bandy, Tammy Wynette and George Jones, Hank Thompson, Jeanie C. Riley, Buck Owens, Little Jimmy Dickens, Conway Twitty, Eddie Rabbit, Johnny Rodriguez, Johnny Paycheck, Lynn Anderson, and Ernest Tubb performed at Schroeder Hall. Mrs. Hoff said, "We can't forget Shoji Tabuchi. I saw his show in Branson, Missouri, and afterwards we met and he remembered playing here."

Roy Clark performed in nearby Victoria, Texas, in 1998 and he paid a visit to Schroeder Hall. "There was Mrs. Hoff" he said, "standing out there looking like a million dollars." Mrs. Hoff recently sold the hall, and the new owners are planning to raise the stage and ceiling to give patrons a better view of the entertainers. They will keep the traditions that the hall has been famous for—hiring the best country and Texas music acts.

Located 15 miles northeast of Goliad at 12514 FM 622. Owners, Les and Rebecca Richter, Dale and Susan Kalinowski, and Jack and Sharon Kleinecke (361-573-7002).

Sealy Opera House

Sealy, Texas ~ Austin County

The Sealy Opera House was built in 1897 by the German Woman's Club. It was destroyed by a storm not too long afterwards and never rebuilt.

Photo courtesy of The County Historic Commission's book:
Dance Halls of Austin County

Sefcik Hall

Seaton, Texas ~ Bell County

Located eight miles east of Temple, Seaton's early history dates back to 1891 when the first post office was established. Officials in Washington, D.C. were responsible for choosing the name Seaton when the community applied for its post office.

Sefcik Hall, pronounced *Chefchick*, was built by Tom Sefcik in 1923. It is now owned by his daughter Alice Sulak, who has managed the hall since 1971. Sunday dances continue on the second floor of the hall, and dancers have made the beautiful preserved hardwood floor creak to polka bands such as Brave Combo and The Praha Brothers. The Dancehall Boys from Austin have been dedicated to keeping the Texas/Czech dance music alive in this part of Texas. Their determination to play Czech music created by their ancestors has kept this music form from becoming extinct.

Seaton is located eight miles east of Temple on Farm Road 53. Sefcik Hall is located just .3 miles from Farm Road 53.

Photo courtesy of Judy Cathey-Treviño

Shady Acres Resort and Dance Hall

New Braunfels, Texas ~ Guadalupe County

Shady Acres Resort, located just outside New Braunfels on Lake Dunlap, was a joint venture between music promoter/fiddler Jett Fellows and country singer George Jones. It opened in 1964 with the purpose of making New Braunfels the center of "hillbilly" entertainment in South Texas, and for the two short years that it was in business, it reached that goal. It had a seating capacity of 1,200 inside and a large outdoor pavilion surrounded by huge oak trees.

Booking agent Jimmie Klein with George Jones
Photo courtesy of Jet Fellows

Jim Reeves and the Blue Boys
Photo courtesy of Jet Fellows

Jet booked many of the top touring acts at the Big "D" Jamboree at the Sportatorium in Dallas, and those performers would travel down Interstate 35 and play Shady Acres. Jim Reeves, Buck Owens, Webb Pierce, Billy Walker, Kitty Wells, Jimmy C. Newman, Hank Snow, Connie Smith, Little Jimmy Dickens, Bill Anderson, Porter Wagoner, Leon Payne, Ernest Tubb (who played for $500), Ray Price (with a show date on April 1, 1965, and payment of $850), Roger Miller (with a guarantee of $500 on August 8, 1964), and Hank Thompson (with two performances on June 17 and 18, 1965, for $1,500) were a few of the acts that made the journey to New Braunfels to play the hall. Jet remembers paying Willie Nelson $150 for a solo performance on the outdoor pavilion.

George Chambers and the Country Gentlemen backed many of these artists. Before George Jones brought in his own band members (band contracts show that he was given $1,000 for a November 19, 1965 date) he used the Country Gentlemen to play behind him as did Don Gibson, Moe Bandy, and Loretta Lynn.

After the hall closed, the 160-acre site was developed into a sub-division, and the building was used as a recreational center. Jet stated that Shady Acres was a fun, wholesome, family place where people loved to come out and hear good country music and dance.

Buck Owens and the Buckaroos

Owens and his lead guitarist/harmony vocalist Don Rich (next to Owens) created a driving "freight train" type of music with their twin Fender Telecaster guitars, which became known as the "Bakersville Sound." A motorcycle accident in 1974 ended Rich's life. *Photo courtesy of Jet Fellows.*

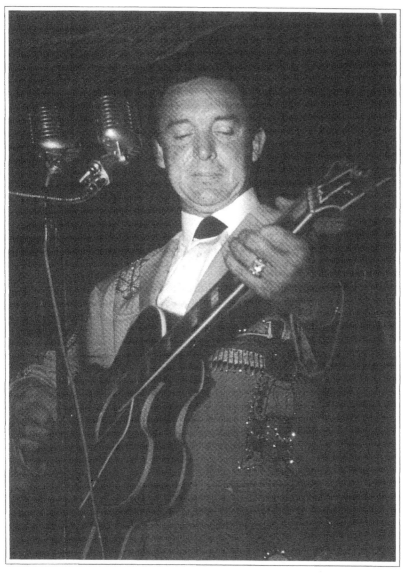

Ray Price performing at Shady Acres, April 1, 1965

Price helped define the 4/4 bass and shuffle rhythm that has been so dominant in country music. His 1956 hit "Crazy Arms" knocked Elvis off the charts. *Photo courtesy of Jet Fellows.*

Silver Spur

Bandera, Texas ~ Bandera County

Bandera in the 1940s and 1950s was a town that resembled some-thing out of the Old West. It was a place to go have fun and let your hair down. The law was lenient towards drunken cowboys and trou-blemakers meandering in town and throwing up on the sidewalks of Main Street. If you could belly up to the bar, you would be served a beer. Dickie Hicks recalls his dad going to town to get a haircut and coming home with a black eye. Law officials looked the other way as Mr. Hicks proceeded to beat the hell out of the troublemaker.

Before the sheriff of Bandera started to clean up the town due to pressure from the community, it was host to three venues that brought the cowboys, cowgirls, and dancers out to enjoy great

Ruins of Silver Spur, 2001
Photo courtesy of Judy Cathey-Treviño

country music. On any given Friday or Saturday night the Cabaret, Mansfield Park, and the Silver Spur drew crowds of a thousand folks to each dance.

The Silver Spur, just west of town, sat on a hill with a majestic view overlooking the Medina River and the Texas Hill Country. It was a beautiful spot to go see Ernest Tubb, Bob Wills, Adolph Hofner, The Texas Top Hands, Walter Kleypas, George Jones, Smiley Whitley, and even big bands. Some people still recall watching Adolph's bus struggle to climb the one-lane country road that led to the Silver Spur, but he always made it there.

The Silver Spur closed down and later burned down in the late 1950s.

Standing: Jimmie Revard, Lucky Ford, Skeet Jasper, and Curly Williams
Seated: Jody Kret, Lloyd Baker, Jay Webber, and Jesse Lee Highsmith
Photo courtesy of Jimmie Revard

Sisterdale Dance Hall

Sisterdale, Texas ~ Kendall County

Sisterdale was founded by Nicolaus Zink in 1847. The dance hall was built around 1890 and has been dormant for many years. The beautiful oak bar is now in the Sisterdale Store across the road from the hall.

Take FM Road 1376 north of Boerne about 13 miles. Sisterdale is located at the junction of FM Roads 1376 and 473. The old hall is directly across from the Sisterdale Store.

Photo courtesy of Judy Cathey-Treviño

Skyline Club

Austin, Texas ~ Travis County

One of Austin's most famous music treasures, whose history goes back to 1946, was torn down in 1989 to make way for road expansion. The Skyline Club, once located on North Lamar Boulevard at Braker Lane, in days before the capital city had the traffic problems of today, definitely has a place in Texas music history. It was the premier music venue in town, hosting some of the top acts in country music. Bob Wills, Marty Robbins, Faron Young, Hank Thompson, Ernest Tubb, Ray Price, Jack Greene, and Hank Snow were just a few of country music's mega stars that performed there. Documents indicate that Elvis Presley sang there on October 6, 1955.

The barn-like structure with a large wooden dance floor was also a popular place for lobbyists from the state capitol to entertain state legislators. Ann Peterson recalls going to Wednesday night dances in 1974 with ten-cent longneck beer specials and free admission for ladies, drawing large crowds of men and women to the club. She remembers that the bands that played at the midweek dances were very good. "We had sort of a pact with the girls that met us there. You were required to dance with the first guy who asked, regardless of what he looked like."

During the late 1970s the building was home to the Soap Creek Saloon and featured the likes of the Fabulous Thunderbirds, Delbert McClinton, Willie Nelson, Asleep at the Wheel, and Jerry Jeff Walker.

The Skyline will always be remembered for hosting the last shows of Hank Williams and later Johnny Horton. Horton, who ironically was married to Williams' widow from his second marriage, Billie Jean Jones, had one of the biggest records of 1959 with "The Battle of New Orleans" and also scored big hits with "Honky-Tonk Man," "Sink the Bismark," and "North to Alaska." He died in a car accident in Milano, Texas, following an engagement at the Skyline on November 5, 1960.

Hank Williams had first performed at the Skyline in 1948 as part of a Louisiana Hayride Tour. The four years that followed his initial performance saw him climb the ladder to become the biggest star in country music, but by the time he returned to Austin he was self-destructing, and it was a gamble to book him anywhere. Williams was on the tail end of a controversial Texas tour that would be his last.

December 19, 1952 newspaper advertisement for Hank Williams' show at the Skyline Club. This was his last public appearance. *Reproduced from the collection of the Austin History Center.*

His first show to kick off his tour began at Cook's Hoe-down Club in Houston, where he was booed off the stage. Several cups of coffee did little to help straighten up the troubled entertainer, and the crowd knew it. On Tuesday, December 16, he could only manage to sing eight to ten songs at Macdona Hall just west of San Antonio. Rusty Locke, bandleader and steel guitarist for The Texas Top Hands and the backup band for the show, stated that he was in real bad shape. According to Colin Escott's biography on Williams, he was scheduled to play at the Sportatorium in Dallas on Wednesday and afterwards went to see Bob Wills perform. He played in Snook, Texas, just southwest of College Station the next night, putting on a decent performance.

Big Bill Lister, who opened many shows for Williams, was his chauffeur on the tour. Lister found the unknown acetate recording of Hank Williams' "Tear in My Beer" that Hank Williams Jr. added vocals to and became a big hit song thirty-six years after his dad had died. Lister said that Hank sang two kinds of songs: sad and pitiful.

Warren Stark, owner of the Skyline until the 1960s and promoter for Hank's Texas tour, billed him as "The Sensational Radio Recording Star" for his December 19th appearance in Austin. Featured on the bill were Charley Adams, Tommie and Goldie Hill, and Billy Walker. The show was sold out. Hank's mother, Lillie, was in the audience that evening, and he seemed to be doing a little better, although he was running a high fever and fighting a lingering cold. Tommie Hill and steel guitarist Jimmy Day joined the house band to perform behind Williams, and he went on to perform two sets.

The best-selling country artist for 1952 would be alive for only thirteen more days. He sang a few songs at an American Federation of Musicians' private Christmas party in Montgomery, Alabama, on December 28th, but he seemed to reach down and give everything he had for his Skyline date. Years later Tommie Hill told country music writer Wiley Alexander that Hank saved the best for last. His last public show was the finest performance he had ever seen Hank give. It was fitting for the Texas tour to have taken place in a state where he still remains so immensely popular. He died on New Years Day 1953 en route to a show in Canton, Ohio. He was only twenty-nine years old.

Sons of Hermann Hall (Lodge 66)

Dallas, Texas ~ Dallas County

Two German immigrants are responsible for founding the Hermann Sons organization in Texas in 1861. The proper name, the Order of the Sons of Hermann in the State of Texas, numbers 155 lodges across the state. It began as a fraternal organization of German Texans wanting protection during a period of anti-German sentiment. The Grand Lodge is located in San Antonio.

Lodge 66 is one of the most active in Texas with a liberal music booking policy focusing on Texas singer/songwriters. The *Dallas*

Popular North Texas honky tonker Tommy Alverson
performs at the Sons of Hermann Hall.
Photo courtesy of Tommy Alverson

Observer Readers Poll voted it "Best Music Venue" and "Best Place
to take a Non-Texan." A new breed of Texas entertainers such as
Tommy Alverson, Clay Blaker, Ed Burleson, Ray Wylie Hubbard, Cor-
nell Hurd, Jack Ingram, Robert Earl Keen, Jimmy LaFave, Gary P.
Nunn, Ponty Bone, Toni Price, Kimmie Rhodes, Charlie and Bruce
Robison, Ronny Spears, Chris Wall, Don Walser, Dale Watson, and
Kelly Willis have mixed their songwriting talents and stage presence
at the hall. Legends such as Asleep at the Wheel, Johnny Bush, Light
Crust Doughboys, Augie Meyers, Ray Price, Leon Rausch, Doug
Sahm, Hank Thompson, and legendary songwriters Guy Clark, Billy

Joe Shaver, and Townes Van Zandt have helped pass the torch over to future legends-to-be.

Built in 1910, Sons of Herman Hall activities are swing dance lessons each Wednesday and an acoustic jam session on Thursdays. Saturday nights feature Texas music acts at the dance hall located upstairs. It has a 500-square-foot hardwood dance floor with seating for up to 350 folks.

Located near downtown Dallas at 3414 Elm (at Exposition) (214-747-4422).

Sons of Hermann Hall – Van Raub Paul Vogt Lodge #234

Fair Oaks Ranch, Texas ~ Bexar County

This ghost town was named for Van Raub Byron, one of the first business entrepreneurs in the community. Records indicate that the Sons of Hermann Lodge was chartered in 1908. Meetings are held the first

Photo courtesy of Judy Cathey-Treviño

Tuesday of each month, and the hall can be rented out for parties.

Van Raub is located twenty-four miles northwest of San Antonio just off Interstate 10 at 8793 Dietz Elkhorn Road.

Specht's Store

Bulverde, Texas ~ Bexar County

Specht's was once a general store that supplied this area, north of San Antonio, with staples and dry goods. Built in 1890 by Henry Specht, it has functioned as a post office, telephone company, and now a restaurant specializing in Texas cuisine and Texas music. Kate Mangold, owner/manager/cook and music director, opened up Specht's Store with her husband Jake in 1985. The store has been in Dodge truck commercials and countless other ads on television due to the famous Texas state flag painted on its tin roof.

Photo courtesy of Judy Cathey-Treviño

The bar inside was in a basement in a house nearby that once served customers during Prohibition. The switchboard that once serviced twenty lines hangs on a wall. It was last used in 1956. The store is small and most folks eat outside on picnic tables where they can also enjoy performances each Saturday night. I released a single titled "I Luv me Trucka" at Specht's Store just before the summer of 1990.

A Specht's Store Special was held in a field west of the store on April 13, 1973. On the bill were Willie Nelson, Pure Prairie League (with Vince Gill in the band), Ray Wylie Hubbard, Sammi Smith, Dale Jackson, Rex Foster, and Augie Meyers and his Western Headband. The food and music at Specht's Store have always been special.

Take Blanco Road north of San Antonio; Specht's is off Blanco Rd.; nine miles north of Loop 1604 at 122 Specht Rd. (830-980-7121). Kate Mangold, owner.

SPJST 80

Holland, Texas ~ Bell County

Holland was settled around 1860 and was originally known as Mountain Home. In 1877 James R. Holland built a steam cotton gin, and later the Missouri, Kansas and Texas Railroad came to the community. The settlement was renamed Holland in 1879.

SPJST 80 was established around 1909 and still hosts bingo and Czech dance bands today.

Located on Farm Road 2268 just a half mile from Highway 95.

SPJST Star Hall

Seaton, Texas ~ Bell County

The original hall, built in 1906, had to be torn down when Highway 53 was widened in 1963. A new hall was built further into the property shortly afterwards. Dorothy Pechal, who works for the SPJST organization in Temple, stated that the original hall had a large stage and beautiful black and gray speckled woodwork surrounding the windows. It was an ideal setting for the many plays performed by various theatrical groups throughout the years. After the new hall was built, several additions were added as the community grew. It continues to serve the area with dances scheduled each week.

Seaton is located eight miles east of Temple on Farm Road 53. SPJST Star Hall is located on 53.

Photo courtesy of Judy Cathey-Treviño

SPJST

Fayetteville, Texas ~ Fayette County

Another fine example of the SPJST halls located across
Central and Southeast Texas.
Photo courtesy of Judy Cathey-Treviño

Stafford Opera House

Columbus, Texas ~ Colorado County

The old Stafford Opera House was built in 1886 by millionaire cattle-
man R.E. Stafford. The stately interior, which seated one thousand,
had gas burning chandeliers and an elaborate hand painted curtain.
Opening performance, *As In a Looking Glass*, starred vaudevil-
lian/singer/actress Lillian Russell. Houdini performed his magic at the
Opera House, and other big-name entertainers of the day played
there also.

The Opera House was host to one of the top western swing
shows in the state, honoring the late Colorado County native son
Shelly Lee Alley, who pioneered western swing and country music on
the radio. Alley, born near Alleyton, Texas, on July 6, 1894, wrote
"Travelin' Blues," which was recorded by Jimmie Rodgers in San
Antonio in 1931. Shelly and his brother Alvin played "twin fiddles" on
the session, and the combination of blues, jazz, and "folk" roots created a new sound that was to be known as "Texas Swing." The style
was to become a major influence on Bob Wills, who took this sound to
new levels. Wills later recorded "Travelin' Blues" as did Gene Autry,
Lefty Frizzell, Ernest Tubb, and Merle Haggard.

The importance of Shelly Lee Alley as a songwriter, performer,
bandleader, and musician cannot be overstated. His pop songs eventually took a new direction when he hesitantly combined them with
"hillbilly" music later in his career. He was a pioneer in commercial
radio when it came to Dallas in 1922 and performed on various radio
programs in the area with his orchestra. He died knowing that some
of his best works were never released or recorded.

Former Texas Playboys Johnny Gimble, Leon Rausch, Herb
Remington, and The Original River Road Boys honored Alley with
performances on June 12, 1999. Also on the show was country music
hall of fame member Floyd Tillman with a special appearance by Cliff
Bruner. Leon "Pappy" Selph was to appear on the bill but passed
away on January 8, 1999. The annual Shelly Lee Alley tribute

outgrew the Opera House and is now celebrated at the Walker County Fairgrounds in Huntsville.

Columbus is 65 miles west of Houston on Interstate 10 and State Highway 71. The Opera House is located in the downtown square area.

Sutherland Springs Dance Pavilion

Sutherland Springs, Texas ~ Wilson County

Founded by Dr. John Sutherland in 1849, its first inhabitants were from Scotland. The citizens of the community divided the town into "New Town" on one side of Cibolo Creek and "Old Town" on the other. Hotel Sutherland opened in 1908 as a resort in "New Town." A 1913 flood destroyed parts of the resort, and the following year a

Dance pavilion at Sutherland Springs Hotel during the time the property was owned by Patillo Higgins. Inscription by Higgins: "Old Pavilion at New Sutherland Springs." Sutherland Springs, Texas, 1940. *Photo courtesy of UT Institute of Texan Cultures at San Antonio, courtesy of Tambria L. Read.*

dance pavilion was added to the existing structure. In the latter part of the 1920s, a flu epidemic, fire, and the Great Depression forced Hotel Sutherland to close. The remaining structure was torn down in 1945, and the wood was salvaged for building material.

Sutherland Springs is on U.S. Highway 87, twenty miles east of San Antonio.

Swiss Alp

Swiss Alp, Texas ~ Fayette County

Egon and Marian Tietjen bought the dance hall in 1946 from Egon's father who had owned it since 1933. Marian said that there was a dance every weekend for forty-five years. Sometimes, on Friday, Saturday, and Sunday evenings, she remembers her father-in-law letting guinea hens loose on the dance floor prior to a dance, and he would let the customers who caught the guineas in for free. They were allowed to take the hens home after the dance. Broom dances were popular at

Photo courtesy of Judy Cathey-Treviño

Adolph Hofner and the Boys (1942)

Standing: Wilbur Beeler (trumpet). Kneeling left to right: Eddie Duncan (steel guitar and bass), Leonard Brown (drums and trumpet), Adolph (guitar and vocals), J.R. Chatwell (fiddle), Rudy Rivera (clarinet), and Ernie LaBoide (piano and accordion). Notice drums on trunk of car. Stand-up bass guitar was always strapped on top. *Photo courtesy of Junior Mitchan.*

Swiss Alp. A man would begin dancing with a broom and tag another man on the shoulder, and the men would trade dance partners. According to Marian, B.J. Thomas ("Raindrops Keep Falling on My Head") started his career at the hall.

Besides B.J. Thomas, one of the most popular bands that performed there during the early 1960s was Roy Head and the Traits, whose song "Treat Her Right" went to number two on both the pop and R&B charts. Other bands that played there were the Emotions, Barons, Cabin Stills and Foxfire, Kross Kountry, and the Velvets. At one time Adolph Hofner played there once a week. The hall could hold around 1,200, but when Bob Wills played there in 1968 with Tag Lambert as his lead singer and backed by the Velvets, a standing room crowd squeezed in to see the "King of Western Swing." "It was so crowded you couldn't even fall down," Marian said.

The hall is about to crumble. Marian stated that she'll probably have it torn down, and with it a chapter of Texas music history will go down in the rubble.

Located on U.S. Highway 77, ten miles south of La Grange.

Texas Dance Hall

Bulverde, Texas ~ Bexar County

The Texas Dance Hall was a short-lived venue that opened in September of 1981 and remained in business for five years. Real estate opportunities were the reason the Archilles family decided to close down the hall. The land and dance hall was sold to Dan Parish for his building supply company.

Located just north of San Antonio on Highway 281, it hosted the top country acts of the 1980s. With a state-of-the-art built-in sound system and a seating capacity of 3,000, it was a real showcase for these performers. Tommy Achilles stated that at the time it also had the largest independent septic system in Texas.

Ray Price was the opening act on September 5, 1981, and was followed by such artists as Ronnie Milsap, George Jones, Jerry Lee Lewis, Johnny Rodriguez, Ernest Tubb, Tammy Wynette, Loretta Lynn, Freddy Fender, Johnny Bush, Merle Haggard, George Strait, Johnny Cash, The Texas Playboys, and the closing act—Willie Nelson.

It was located 10 miles north of San Antonio International Airport on U.S. Highway 281, on the left.

Courtesy of
Action Magazine

Johnny Cash and Ray Sczepanik, Texas Dance Hall, October 21, 1982

Ray Sczepanik promoted shows with many of the top stars in country music. He booked Johnny Cash, Hank Thompson, Merle Haggard, Ernest Tubb, Ray Price, and a young star-to-be George Strait. Ray still has contracts showing Strait playing at Pat's Hall, The Broken Spoke, The Cabaret, and Texas Dance Hall. Strait was making around $2,500 per engagement and was paid $15,000 for his December 31, 1983 New Years show at Texas Dance Hall. It was the most money he had ever made at the time. *Photo courtesy of Ray Sczepanik.*

Texas Star Inn

Leon Valley, Texas ~ Bexar County

On a hill overlooking Leon Valley, the Texas Star Inn was host to many great country stars. Photos of Ernest Tubb, Hank Williams, and Willie Nelson hung at the entrance of the hall. Other artists that performed there were Roger Miller, Faron Young, Ray Price, Johnny Bush, and fiddler/singer/songwriter Allen "Slim" Roberts, who came to Texas in 1950 with the Tex Ritter band. It was suggested by owner Frank "Papa" Klein that John Bush Shinn drop his last name and use Johnny Bush as his new moniker. "Papa" Klein hired him to play in 1954, which became Bush's debut into the country music business. His self-penned "Whiskey River," a song that Willie Nelson opens every show with, went gold, as did Willie's "You Ought to See Me Cry" recorded by Bush.

The Texas Star Inn was built in 1946 and purchased by Papa Klein and his wife in the early 1950s. The two-story rock building, with a

Photo courtesy of Judy Cathey-Treviño

300 seating capacity and a 6,000-square-foot dance floor, was a permanent home for Papa and his band The Texas Star Playboys. The band performed until the early 1960s and appeared on KEYL-TV (now KENS) from 1951 to 1953. Singer/guitarist Klein sold the Texas Star Inn in 1979 to Polly Herschberger, Gene Patton, and Dodie Sullivan. In the mid-1980s Polly and Lorene Luckey took over ownership of the hall. Part of the movie *Waltz Across Texas* was filmed there. The hall closed in 1993 and reopened as Grady's Bar-B-Que a short time later.

The Texas Star Inn (Grady's) is located at 7400 Bandera Road in Leon Valley, a town northwest of San Antonio.

Tin Hall Dance Hall and Saloon

Cypress, Texas ~ Harris County

The community of Cypress was settled by Germans in the 1840s. A dance hall was first built in 1878 but later burned down. With help

Photo courtesy of Judy Cathey-Treviño

from the Cypress Gun and Rifle Club, a new hall was constructed using corrugated tin for its outside structure. It became a place for dairy farmers to meet in 1890. In the 1920s an upstairs was added to the building, and the dance floor was built then. The dance floor on the second level is 4,100 square feet, and the hall can accommodate about 1,200 people. Tin Hall is 12,000 square feet. Its "island bar" is one of the largest found in any dance hall.

Tin Hall is the oldest entertainment complex in Harris County and is owned by Fred Stockton, great-grandson of one of the founding families. Merle Haggard, Willie Nelson, Clyde Brewer and The Original River Road Boys, Pappy Selph, Bob Dunn, and Asleep at the Wheel have performed at the hall with more recent shows by Ray Price, Hank Thompson, Gene Watson, Don Williams, Earl Thomas Conley, Johnny Rodriguez, Hank Williams III, Pat Green, and The Bellamy Brothers. Tin Hall is located five minutes east of U.S. Highway 290 at 14800 Huffmeister Road, in Cypress, Texas (northwest of Houston). It is open for concerts only (713-664-7450).

The Trio Club

Mingus, Texas ~ Palo Pinto County

Named after early settler William Mingus, this community developed with the building of the Texas and Pacific railway in 1881. Two miles south of Mingus is the ghost town of Thurber, which at one time had a population close to 10,000, between 1918 and 1920. The bituminous coal mining business, responsible for the population explosion, eventually folded and led to Thurber's decline.

The Trio Club in Mingus, named for the three men who ran it, was built in 1952. Frank Belinski, Edward "Snake" Dumoth, and Albert Abraham managed the hall from 1952 to 1995.

Some well-known names that played there were Bob Wills, Tony Douglas, and Jody Nix. Linda May and her husband, Joe, now own the Trio Club and have Saturday dances and a Sunday matinee dance each week. "The bands we book play country and western and old country music. I've had Marty Stuart and Gary Stewart at the hall, and Jody Nix still performs here," said Linda.

The 6,000-square-foot long narrow building is made of red brick and has a half dome roof. The stage area is deep but not very wide. This is one of the oldest halls in this part of Texas.

It is located approximately 50 miles west of Fort Worth. From Interstate 20 take FM 108 in Thurber and go two miles north to Mingus (254-672-5664).

Photo courtesy of Judy Cathey-Treviño

Turner Hall

Fredericksburg, Texas ~ Gillespie County

The Texas Historical Commission has a plaque out front that reads:
Fredericksburg Social Turn Verein

The Fredericksburg Turn Verein was established in 1871
in the tradition of German gymnastic clubs. Initially
located at a site nearby, the club opened with a gymnastics
school and a nine-pin bowling alley. In 1872 the club held
the first of its annual Christmas celebrations and in 1883
sponsored a fire brigade which became the city volunteer
fire department. The Turn Verein moved to this location in
1909. Children's gymnastics, Christmas celebrations and
bowling continue at Fredericksburg Social Verein, one of
the oldest continuing organizations in the city.

Photo courtesy of Judy Cathey-Treviño

Since 1989 the Verein has held fund raisers to help restore the interior of the hall. A pork barbecue dinner is served each year with proceeds directed for maintenance of the hall.

Fredericksburg is located on U.S. Highway 290, seventy miles west of Austin. To find Turner Hall take Main Street going west. Take a right on Adams Street and go three blocks, take a left at the stop sign (Travis Street), and the hall is on your left.

Twin Sisters Dance Hall

Twin Sisters, Texas ~ Blanco County

Several years ago Scott Thompson decided to spend his New Year's Eve at the annual dance at Twin Sisters Hall and had heard that he must buy his tickets for his group before that evening. The afternoon before the dance, he strolled into the hall and asked if he could

Photo courtesy of Judy Cathey-Treviño

Ray Benson and Asleep at the Wheel

"Western Swing music isn't dead, it's just asleep at the wheel." Ray Benson has kept the tradition of Bob Wills' music alive with his award winning band, Asleep at the Wheel. With eight Grammy awards under their belt, they continue to spread their music throughout the world. Twin Sisters is one of Ray's favorite old halls. *Photo courtesy of Ray Benson.*

purchase his tickets in advance. Two elderly ladies and a man around the age of eighty-five were handling ticket sales. They told Scott that his party must be present so that they could staple the tickets to their collar and that this was always the policy before the New Year's Eve dance. Scott politely asked if they could bend the rules a little and allow him to take the tickets with him, which they gave him permission to do. As he was leaving he noticed that he should also reserve a table for his party. He walked back to the three and asked what their policy for reserving a table would be. "You need to come early and just grab a spot." Well, this was a great inconvenience and he asked if they could bend the rules again and allow him to reserve a table in advance. The three huddled together, and after discussing the situation they gave him approval to reserve his table. This is what makes these honky-tonks so unique. The fact that there has been little change in the way these dance halls have functioned over the years just keeps with the tradition.

Twin Sisters Dance Hall is named after Twin Sisters Mountains, which can be seen at a distance. The first written accounting of a dance at the hall dates back to 1898. The hall was built in 1870. In German script the record gives detailed expenses incurred by the hall. Band-$20.00; 16 kegs of beer and 24 cases of soda were sold for a total gross of 74.80.

In 1929 records indicate that the band was paid $60.

The Twin Sisters Hall Club operates the facility, and every first Saturday of the month there is a dance. The hall closes in January and February of each year and once hosted dances for trailriders while en route to the San Antonio Livestock Show and Rodeo. Each December in addition to the monthly dance, they celebrate a Christmas and New Year's Eve Dance. Seating capacity around 500 (830-833-4808).

VFW Post 8918

Circleville, Texas ~ Williamson County

Located on Highway 95 just north of Circleville.

Photo courtesy of Judy Cathey-Treviño

Waring General Store and Dance Hall

Waring, Texas ~ Kendall County

Built in 1900 by Herman Rust.

Take Interstate 10 west from Boerne to Farm Road 1621 (three miles south of Comfort). Take a right and go five miles. The General Store will be on your left.

Photo courtesy of Judy Cathey-Treviño

Weesatche Dance Hall

Weesatche, Texas ~ Goliad County

The town of Weesatche was first known as Middletown due to its location between Goliad and Clinton. Residents renamed the town after the huisache tree when there became some confusion with another Middletown in Comal County.

Located in northern Goliad County, Olde Weesatche Hall closed in 1983 but has come back to life as the Olde Middletown Cafe and Bar. Built by Otto Luedicke around 1919, it had rows of seats around three of the open sides that were separated from the floor by chicken wire. Adam Schaeffer closed in the hall in 1937. Betty Straus purchased the hall in 1998 and has scheduled weekly dances in addition to serving food at the cafe in the hall.

Weesatche is located thirteen miles north of Goliad on State Highway 119. The hall is just off 119 on Farm Road 884.

Photo courtesy of Judy Cathey-Treviño

Weinheimer Dance Hall

Stonewall, Texas ~ Gillespie County

Built by Alvin H. Weinheimer in the 1920s, the structure was first an open-air pavilion before being enclosed shortly afterwards. The drop-down curtain still has the ads marketing local businesses in the immediate area. Benches were permanently built around the inside of the hall. It was used for dances, community fairs, reunions, school functions, and also as a church. It was used for storage for many years.

On October 12, 2001, a devastating storm hit Stonewall. The old dance hall was brought to the ground by a tornado that also destroyed and damaged several homes in the same area of Ranch Road 1. In less than fifteen minutes a piece of history was gone.

It was located on Ranch Road 1 in Stonewall.

Photo courtesy of Judy Cathey-Treviño

Welcome Mannerchor Hall

Industry, Texas ~ Austin County

The Welcome Mannerchor, a German male singing group, was organized in 1889. The group used Welcome Hall, built in 1899, for rehearsals and performances. The architect for the hall, Professor A.A. Baring, was also the director of the singing group. The hall was the centerpiece for dances and plays and was later used as a meeting

Photo courtesy of Judy Cathey-Treviño

place for the Hermann Sons Lodge. Some of the groups who performed there in addition to the "Mannerchor" were the Welcome Brass Band and Lindy's Brass Band.

Milton Huebner purchased Welcome Hall in 1980, after it had remained dormant for many years, and restored the facility to its former grandeur. It was moved from the town site of Welcome to five miles north of Industry, Texas, and has become a popular place for weddings. Ann Lindemann from Industry said that almost every weekend is booked for a wedding celebration.

Industry is located on State Highway 159 just northeast of Fayetteville.

Wessel's Store and Dance Hall

Rutersville, Texas ~ Fayette County

My journey through southeast Texas came to a sudden stop as I drove through Rutersville. I noticed what appeared to be an old dilapidated dance hall with windows shut tight and in need of repair. The only business in town was a truck accessory company, so I walked in to ask if anyone could tell me something about the old building. I was directed to the owner of the business, Mr. Kurt Tietjen. He recalled with fondness what the hall was like during its glory years. He remembered sitting on his front porch as a young boy and listening to bands play during the 1920s. Later he attended dances and always enjoyed seeing Adolph Hofner perform. The store and dance hall have been closed for some time, but with a little imagination you can still hear Adolph singing a honky-tonk song.

Rutersville is located on State Highway 159, five miles east of La Grange.

Photo courtesy of Judy Cathey-Treviño

Wied Hall

Wied, Texas ~ Lavaca County

Wied Hall is on Farm Road 1891, just north of U.S. Highway 90A, midway between Hallettsville and Shiner.

Photo courtesy of Judy Cathey-Treviño

Smaller Venues Promoting Texas Music

It would be unfair to omit some of the smaller venues that have made it their goal to keep Texas music alive. With Nashville going in another direction, marketing more of a pop sound of country and getting further away from traditional country music, a horde of Texas artists have dedicated themselves to getting back to the roots of country music.

Blaine's Pub in San Angelo is one of these places. Blaine Martin opened his business in 1997. The aura of this town, its people, and its gateway to West Texas makes it easy to understand why Ernest Tubb enjoyed living there so much. Tubb's E & E Tavern was once located a block away from Blaine's. "There's no such thing as a drunk at Blaine's, just a satisfied customer," is their motto. Stop by and enjoy the great music at 10 Harris Street.

Casbeers, located on 1719 Blanco Road in San Antonio, was built in 1932 by Newt Casbeer as a full-service bar. In 1999 Steve Silbas and Barbara Wolfe took over Casbeers and added original live music to its menu. Known for serving some of the best enchiladas in the city, it is becoming very well known for the entertainment as well. The Texas Tornados filmed their video *Is Anybody Going to San Antone?* at this quaint neighborhood bar in 1991. Each year in November Casbeers hosts a Doug Sahm Memorial Tribute with proceeds used to make improvements on youth baseball fields and for a ballpark to be named in his honor.

On the edge of the most elite neighborhoods in Houston (River Oaks) is another bar that has catered to great Texas music artists. **Blanco's Bar & Grill**, located at 3406 W. Alabama, has music every Thursday and Friday with special events held throughout the year.

Cheatham Street Warehouse, located in San Marcos, opened in June 1974 by Kent Finlay and Jim Cunningham for the purpose of promoting Texas songwriters. It was during this peak of the country progressive era that such acts as B.W. Stevenson, Guy Clark, Billy Joe Shaver, Asleep at the Wheel, Jerry Jeff Walker, Willie Nelson, Ray Wylie Hubbard, Augie Meyers, and George Strait came to Cheatham Street. Strait and his Ace in the Hole Band played their very first jobs there. A graduate of Southwest Texas University, Strait has been a leading proponent of western swing and traditional country music. Born in Poteet, he has become one of country music's brightest stars, winning eleven Country Music Association Awards. After a few years absence, Finlay has returned to help develop new songwriters and to bring back some of the Cheatham Street alumni. Located at 119 Cheatham Street.

Thirty miles west of Austin in Spicewood on Highway 71 is a roadhouse that is owned by Randy "Poodie" Locke. Poodie has been Willie Nelson's stage manager for close to thirty years. Rusty Wier, Billy Joe Shaver, and Ray Wylie Hubbard perform there regularly. Willie Nelson and Merle Haggard have performed there three separate times. **Poodie's Hilltop Bar** is located at 22308 Highway 71 West.

James Curtis Riley may not be a name one would readily know, but he holds the distinction of obtaining the first beer license in Texas. South of San Marcos along York Creek is an old building built in the mid-1800s that was once known as the Galloway Saloon. The community of Hunter was a busy spot in Texas when Riley camped out on the steps of the state capitol to get a beer license in September of 1933. Farming and ranching added to a healthy economy around Hunter, and after the Missouri-Pacific Railroad became a stopping point, **Riley's Tavern** became a popular place for locals to go. Riley ran the tavern for fifty-eight years. Rick Wilson has taken over ownership and has hosted former members of the Texas Playboys, Augie Meyers, and other fine Texas talent. Traveling a few miles south of San Marcos, take exit 196 off Interstate 35 west and go one mile and Riley's will be on your left.

Roadies

One of the most important and unheralded duties in a band is that of a "roadie." A roadie wears many hats and performs umpteen jobs that are crucial in keeping a band running efficiently. The most famous of all and known as the "world's oldest roadie" is Ben Dorcy III. Born in 1925 in San Antonio, Ben, affectionately known as "Lovie," is your typical sidekick companion who has worked with many of the top entertainers in country music. Whether it be fetching coffee, driving the bus, washing the bus, or carrying the star's guitar, their role is as vital as any musician in the band.

A character similar to Gabby Hayes, Dorcy started his career working for Larry Nolen and not long afterwards joined Hank Thompson. Stints with Ray Price and Willie Nelson followed. While traveling to the movie set *The Alamo* in Brackettville with Spud Goodall and his band, he was introduced to John Wayne and immediately went to

John Wayne, Ben Dorcy III, and Maureen O'Hara, San Antonio, late 1950s
Photo courtesy of Ben Dorcy III

. Ben Dorcy III and Merle Haggard, February 9, 1998, San Antonio
Photo courtesy of Ben Dorcy III

work for him as a valet of sorts. Ben seldom left the Duke's sight. Once while actors and actresses were gathered for supper, he and Wayne appeared together on the horizon overlooking the crewmembers and actors. As Wayne packed his cigarettes and slowly pulled one out, Ben was by his side to light his cigarette. With the crew watching from down below Ben proceeded to singe John Wayne's nose hairs as he miscalculated the flame on his Zippo lighter.

Ben has been a loyal employee to everyone he has worked with. Waylon Jennings even wrote a song about Ben's never ending love in taking care of him while on the road.

As an off-duty fireman, Jesse Ochoa started out doing security backstage at music concerts at the old convention arena in San Antonio. He became a limo driver/bodyguard, taking care of such stars as Julio Iglesias, George Strait, Tanya Tucker, The Rolling Stones, Los Lobos, and most recently Charlie Robison. He was named road manager for Flaco Jimenez, and this lead him to the job of tour manager for the Texas Tornados.

Whether it is helping unload or load music equipment, tune guitars, or to oversee room accommodations, these little-known individuals are there to take care of the star.

Left to right: Louie Ortega, Augie Meyers, Flaco Jimenez,
Jesse Ochoa, Lee Roy Parnell in Zurich, Switzerland
Photo courtesy of Jesse Ochoa

Sources

Introduction

Jan Hardwig "The Past, Present and Future of Polka Music—America's Ethnic Music Mantle," *The Austin Chronicle*, October 30-November 5, 1998

"Country Music, The Texas Connection," *Houston Chronicle*, September 30, 1979, page 9

Country—The Music and the Musicians From the Beginnings to the '90s, Country Music Foundation, Abbeville Press

Barry McCloud, *Country Music and its Performers*, Perigee Books (The Berkley Publishing Group)

Chester Rosson, *Texas Monthly: Texas Music Source*, May 1997

Jean-Jacques Peters (Ebu), *The History of Television*

Gene Fowler and Bill Crawford, *Border Radio*, Texas Monthly Press, 1987, page 174

Kevin Coffey, *Biography on Shelly Lee Alley*

Nolan Porterfield, *Jimmie Rodgers: The Life and Times of America's Blue Yodler*

Cary Ginell with special assistance by Roy Lee Brown, *Milton Brown and the Founding of Western Swing* (Univ. of Illinois Press)

Charles R. Townsend, *San Antonio Rose—The Life and Music of Bob Wills* (Univ. of Illinois Press)

Official web site of Rock and Roll Hall of Fame, www.rockhall.com

Peter Guralnick, *Searching for Robert Johnson*

Kevin Coffey, liner notes on *The Daffan Records Story*

Kevin Coffey, *Ted Daffan's Official Biography*

Ted Daffan's performance set list

Frankie McWhorter, *Cowboy Fiddler in Bob Wills' Band* (Texas Tech University Press, 1992)

Ronnie Pugh, *Ernest Tubb, The Texas Troubadour* (Duke Univ. Press)

Kevin Coffey, *Western Swing Journal,* issue 12, page 24

Daniel Cooper, *Lefty Frizzell—The Honky-Tonk Life of Country Music's Greatest Singer* (Little, Brown and Co.)

Official biography of Ray Price

Robert K. Obermann, *A Century of Country—An Illustrated History of Country Music* (TV Books)

Horace Logan with Bill Sloan, *Louisiana Hayride Years* (St. Martins Griffin, 1999)

Official web site of George Jones, www.georgejones.com

Michael Corcoran, "The Ghost of Harry Choates," *Austin American Statesman*, July 17, 2001

Willie Nelson with Bud Shrake, *Willie—An Autobiography* (Pocket Books)

Christopher Gray, "Live at Gilley's—The Mother of All Honky-Tonks," *Austin Chronicle*, October 15, 1999

Colin Escott, *Hank Williams—The Biography* (Little, Brown and Co.)

Jim Beal Jr., "Country's Cool," *San Antonio Express-News*

Texas Music Industry Directory

Dance Halls

Dance Halls of Austin County, the Austin County Historical Commission

Kathleen Bauer, "Settlement and Progress of the Albert Community," *Junior Historian*, September 1968

The Handbook of Texas Online (THOTO); THOTO is a joint project of the general libraries at the University of Texas at Austin and the Texas State Historical Association.

Atlas of the World (Washington: National Geographic Society, 1963; 5th edition 1981), New Braunfels Zeitung, August 21, 1952

History of Anhalt, the Germania Farmers Verein

Pamphlet, biography on Arkey Blue

Paula Allen, "Davenport Taken," *San Antonio Express-News*, September 28, 1997

Documents of the history of Bracken, Texas

Jerry Needham, "It's to the Bat Cave for Tons of Nutrients," *San*

Antonio Express-News, February 16, 1997

Documents from Blumenthal Farms

Official Broken Spoke web site, www.lnstar.net/bspoke

THOTO — Jeff Carroll. Bibliography: Frank Lotto, *Fayette County: Her History and Her People* (Schulenburg, Texas: Sticker Steam Press 1902; rpt., Austin: University of Texas Press, 1981)

Official Texas Historical Markers (OTHM) State of Texas, Texas Historical Commission, Austin, Texas. These markers provided useful information for this book.

THOTO — Robert H. Thonhoff, *History of Karnes County* (M.A. thesis, Southwest Texas State College, 1963). Vertical files, Barker Texas History Center, University of Texas at Austin (Karnes Co., Texas)

Herman Lehmann, *Nine Years Among the Indians 1870-1879* (University of New Mexico Press)

Peter Guralnick and Ernst Jorgensen, *Elvis Day by Day* (New York: Ballantine Books, 1999)

Brochure from Clear Springs Catfish Restaurant

Official web site of Coupland Dance Hall, www.couplaninn.com/dancehall.html

Jay Hardwig, *Austin Chronicle*, Vol. 117, issue 33

THOTO — Bibliography: Patrick Abbott and C.M. Woodruff eds., *The Balcones Escarpment: Geology, Hydrology, Ecology* (San Antonio: Geological Society of America, 1986). Edward Collins and Stephen Lauback, *Faults and Fractures in the Balcones Fault Zone* (Austin: Austin Geological Society, 1990). Robert T. Hill, "The Geologic Evolution of the Non-Mountainous Topography of the Texas Region: An Introduction to the Study of the Great Plains," *American Geologist* 10 (August 1892). E. H. Sellards, W. S. Adkins, and F. B. Plummer, *The Geology of Texas* (University of Texas Bulletin 3232, 1932)

San Antonio Express-News

Band contracts from the Farmer's Daughter

THOTO — Daniel P. Green. Bibliography: Oscar Haas, *History of New Braunfels and Comal County, Texas 1844-1944* (Austin: Steck, 1968)

John Morthland, "Come Dancing," *Texas Monthly*, March 1995, page 85

Official biography of Floore Country Store, *History of Floore Country Store*

THOTO — Nellie Murphree. Bibliography: Nellie Murphree, *A History of DeWitt County* (Victoria, Texas, 1962)

THOTO — Martin Donell Kohout. Bibliography: Gillespie County Historical Society, *Pioneers in God's Hills* (2 Vols. Austin: Von Boeckmann-Jones, 1960, 1974) Cynthia Hohenberger, "The Grapetown Legacy," *Junior Historian*, September 1965

Official web site of Gruene Hall, www.gruenehall.com

THOTO — Jeff Carroll. Bibliography: Terry G. Jordan, *German Seed in Texas Soil: Immigrant farmers in Nineteenth-Century Texas* (Austin: University of Texas Press, 1966)

THOTO — Richard Bruhn. Bibliography: *Dallas Morning News*, November 4, 1965. John Moursund, *Blanco County Families for One Hundred Years* (Austin, 1958). *Blanco County History* (Burnet, Texas: Nortex, 1979)

Official biography on Kendalia Halle, *History of Kendalia Halle*

THOTO — Ed Janecka. Bibliography: John Janacek, *St. Cyril and Methodius—Diamond Jubilee, 1877-1952, Dubina, Texas* (second ed., Yorktown, Texas, DeWitt County View, 1979). La Grange High School, *Fayette County: Past and Present* (La Grange, Texas, 1976). Clint Machann, ed., *The Czechs in Texas* (College Station: Texas A&M University Department of English, 1979)

THOTO — Jeff Carroll. Bibliography: Mary Hinton, *Weimer Texas: First 100 Years, 1873-1973* (Austin: Von Boeckmann-Jones, 1973). Frank Lotto, *Fayette County: Her History and Her People* (Schulenburg, Texas Sticker Strem Press, 1902, rpt., Austin: University of Texas Press, 1981)

THOTO — Louis J. Polansky and David S. Walkup. Bibliography: Frank Lotto, *Fayette County: Her History and Her People* (Schulenburg, Texas Sticker Steam Press, 1902, rpt., Austin: University of Texas Press, 1981). Leonie Rummel Weyand and Houston Wade, *An Early History of Fayette County* (La Grange, Texas: LaGrange Journal, 1936)

THOTO — Carole E. Christian. Bibliography: Annie Maud Avis, ed., *History of Burton* (Burton, Texas 1974)

The Cuero Record, Wednesday, October 29, 1997

THOTO — Vivian Elizabeth Smyrl. Bibliography: Malvin George Bowden, *History of Burnet County* (M.A. thesis, University of Texas, 1940). Sandy Bridges, "Longhorn Cavern State Park," *Texas Highways*, July 1986. Victor S. Craun, "Commercial Caves of Texas, in *The Caves of Texas*" (*National Speleological Society Bulletin* 10, April 1948). William H. Matthews III, *The Geologic Story of Longhorn Cavern* (Austin: Bureau of Economic Geology, University of Texas, 1963)

Jan Fritz article with Geronimo Treviño III

Castroville Historical Association

THOTO — Ruben E Ochoa. Bibliography: Castro Colonies Heritage Association, *The History of Medina County Texas* (Dallas: National ShareGraphics, 1983). Houston B. Eggen, *History of Public Education in Medina County, Texas, 1848-1928* (M.A. thesis, University of Texas, 1950)

THOTO — Charles Christopher Jackson. Bibliography: Rudolph L. Biesele, *The History of the German Settlements in Texas, 1831-1861* (Austin: Von Boeckmann-Jones, 1930; rpt. 1964)

THOTO — Christopher Long. Bibliography: Austin County: *Beilage Zum Bellville Wochenblatt den alten Texanern gewidmet und den jungen Texanern zu Butz und Frommen* (Bellville, Texas: Bellville Wochenblatt, 1899)

THOTO — Craig H. Roell. Bibliography: Alfreda Huck, *Our Town, Nordheim, Texas: 75th Anniversary* (Nordheim, Texas, 1972). Nellie Murphree, *A History of DeWitt County* (Victoria, Texas, 1962). Vertical files, Barker Texas History Center, University of Texas Austin

THOTO — Louann Atkins Temple. Bibliography: T. Lindsay Baker, *The First Polish Americans: Silesian Settlements in Texas* (College Station: Texas A&M University Press, 1979). *Dallas Morning News*, September 30, 1988. Edward J. Dworaczyk, "The Millennium History of Panna Maria, Texas (1966)" *Bandera Country*, Spring/Summer 1999

History of Nelson City Dance Hall, Jerry Tilley

THOTO — Mark Odintz. Bibliography: Castro Colonies Heritage Association, *The History of Medina County, Texas* (Dallas: National ShareGraphics, 1983)

THOTO — Vivian Elizabeth Smyrl. Bibliography: Mary Starr Barkley, *History of Travis County and Austin, 1839-1899* (Waco: Texian Press, 1963). John L. German and Myron Janzen, *Texas Post Offices by County, 1986*

Stanley Oberst and Lori Torrance, *Elvis in Texas: The Undiscovered King 1954-1958* (Plano: Republic of Texas Press, 2002)

Sons of Hermann Hall (Dallas) web site, www.sonsofhermann.com

Texas Ghost Towns web site, www.texasghosttowns.com

San Antonio Light, December 13, 1981

Official web site of Tin Hall, www.tinhall.com

Third Coast Music "The Big D Jamboree," #36/125, January 2000

San Antonio Express-News, June 23, 2000

Henry Wolff Jr., *Victoria Advocate*, December 3, 1998

Del-Voda Harris and Joy Mygrants, "History of a Texas Landmark," *Victoria Advocate*, October 28, 2001

THOTO — Thomas W. Cutter. Bibliography: Daughters of the Republic of Texas, *Founders and Patriots of the Republic of Texas* (Austin, 1963). Daughters of the Republic of Texas, *Master of the Texas Revolution* (Austin, 1986). William DeRyee and R.E. Moore, *The Texas Album of the Eighth Legislature, 1860* (Austin: Miner, Lambert and Perry, 1860). Sam Houston Dixon and Louis Wiltz Kemp, *The Heroes of San Jacinto* (Houston: Anson Jones, 1932). *Memorial and Genealogical Record of Southwest Texas* (Chicago: Goodspeed, 1894: rpt., Easley, South Carolina: Southern Historical Press 1978). Texas House of Representatives, *Biographical Directory of the Texan Conventions and Congresses, 1832-1845* (Austin: Book Exchange, 1941). Gifford E. White, *1830 Citizens of Texas* (Austin: Eakin, 1983)

THOTO — James and Ann Lindemann. Bibliography: Rudolph L. Biesele, *The History of the German Settlements in Texas, 1831-1861* (Austin: Von Boeckmann-Jones, 1930, rpt. 1964). Terry G. Jordan, *German Seed in Texas Soil: Immigrant Farmers in Nineteenth-Century Texas* (Austin: University of Texas Press, 1966). Ann and James Lindemann, eds., *Historical Accounts of*

Industry, Texas (New Ulm, Texas, 1986)

The Blues Café Web Site

Joe Carr and Alan Munde, *Prairie Nights to Neon Lights* (Texas Tech University Press, 1995)

Interviews

Roy Lee Brown
Adolph Hofner
Junior Mitchan
Bob Davis
Geronimo Treviño Jr.
Cliff Bruner
Wiley Alexander
Caesare Masse
Steve Laughlin
Jewell Chatwell
Grant Boatright
Bruce Channel
Hank Harrison
Randy "Poodie" Locke
Augie Meyers
Bernice Weinheimer
Harvey Schaefer
Robert Earl Keen
John Oaks
Evelyn Carolan
Mrs. Charles Suetik
Anton Vrasel
George Chambers
Ray Sczepanik
David Zettner
Jayson Fritz
William Ilse
Wilton Crider
Helen Ferguson
Ruby Deike
Mrs. Leroy Field
Rusty Locke

Buzz Morganstern
Leonard Moore
Rick Garza
Slim Coleman
Dorothy Daffan Yannuzzi
Doyle Weber
Don Pack
Jerry Grote
Louis J. Polansky
Debbie Cole
Craig Herman
Peggy Wood
Bob Saulle
Roy Clark
Helen Hoff
Ann Peterson
Kate Mangold
Dorothy Pechal
Shelly Lee Alley Jr.
Marian Tietjen
Linda May
Scott Thompson
Ann Lindemann
Kurt Tietjen
Ben Dorcy III
Jesse Ochoa
Willie Nelson
Jet Fellows
Ray Benson
Floyd Tillman
Clyde Brewer

Index